Balanced Life
and Leadership Excellence

Balanced Life

and Leadership Excellence

A Nurturing Relationship

By
Madan Birla

With Cecilia Miller Marshall, Ph.D.

A Publication of
The Balance Group
Memphis

Library of Congress: 97-71401

ISBN: 0-9657644-0-0

Published in the United States by:
The Balance Group
Suite 104
1160 West Poplar Avenue
Collierville, TN 38017

$11.95 U.S., $16.95 Canada

Book design by Beverly Cruthirds, Cruthirds Design
Cover photograph by Steve Cook
Edited by Robert Kerr

To Shashi, Naveen and Manisha
— who make my life journey
fun and worthwhile

Acknowledgments

Many sincere thanks to Sally Thomason, Ed Hirsch, Bill Henson and Jill Johnson-Piper for their insight and contribution, to Terri DePriest for typing and retyping the manuscript, to graphic designer Beverly Cruthirds for her creative shaping of the book, and to Robert Kerr for editing the manuscript and managing the book's production.

We would also like to express our heartfelt gratitude to our families and dear friends for their love and support.

— The author and co-author

About the Author and Co-author

Author Madan Birla, a successful business executive, husband, father, educator and counselor, is uniquely qualified to write this book. It is based on the Effective Leadership and Balanced Life seminar he has been conducting for six years.

He has done graduate work in engineering, business and counseling at the Illinois Institute of Technology, Butler University and the University of Memphis, respectively. Mr. Birla has more than 20 years of management experience at RCA and Federal Express. He is the recipient of the Five Star Award for managerial excellence at Federal Express.

Being a product of two different cultures — East and West — his philosophy combines the best of both and makes compatible what to many people are opposite worlds: business and family. Mr. Birla lives with his wife and two children in Collierville, Tennessee.

• • •

Co-author Dr. Cecilia Miller Marshall, Ph.D., is a licensed psychologist in private practice in Oxford, Mississippi. Educated at Rhodes College, the University of Louisville, and the University of Mississippi, she has 20 years experience in individual and family counseling. Her family includes her husband, two daughters, a dog and two horses.

Contents

Introduction

The decade of the Nineties has been called "the search for balanced life decade." Baby Boomers, after achieving career success and affluence, are now searching for ways to lead balanced lives and enjoy their success.

This book explores the question: *If we all so strongly feel the need and understand the importance of leading a balanced lifestyle — then why aren't more of us doing it?*

A popular and memorable act on the old Ed Sullivan television show in the Fifties and Sixties was a nimble juggler who stacked dozens of spinning dinner plates on tall whirling poles. To the frenetic strains of the musical accompaniment, the performer would lunge from pole to pole, giving each another saving spin just in the nick of time — all the while stacking the plates higher and higher.

The audience — knowing something had to give eventually — trembled with rising anticipation of a spectacular crash. However, just seconds before it seemed the plates were all about to come tumbling down, the juggler would deftly snatch each one from the tops of the poles and take a theatrical bow.

• • •

If that's the way your life feels, this book is for you.

• • •

Some days it takes all our concentration, all our strength and all our speed simply to keep everything from crashing into a million pieces. But how long can we keep it up?

Suppose ... we just stopped spinning?

The plates would crash and break, of course. But after that, what other consequences could we expect? Ed Sullivan might never ask us back, true. However, we could anticipate a welcome silence and a tremendous sense of relief that the manic juggling act was over. We might even glue some of the broken pieces back together and start over in a healthier, more balanced way.

The goal of this book is to help you restore the balance in your life. No matter how "normal" your own juggling act has come to seem, the time-starved human being within longs for balance and equilibrium.

This book will guide you through the Balanced Life Four-Step Process to help you restore your equilibrium. The steps involve:

1. Visualizing the balanced healthy state and taking charge of your life balance.

2. Identifying the root causes of imbalance in your environment — the internal as well as the external causes.

3. Developing a personal action plan to address the root causes identified in Step Two.

4. Taking action to implement the plan.

The first chapter, *The Unbalanced Life: Balanced Life Concerns Are Not Unique to You,* explains that you are not alone. In a survey conducted for the recruiting firm Robert Half International, 56 percent of the men polled said they would give up as much as a quarter of their salary to have more family or personal time.

Asked to select the most important goal for the women's movement today, participants in a TIME/CNN poll rated "helping women balance work and family" as number one.

The second chapter, *Visualizing the Balanced Healthy State and Balanced Life Four-Step Process,* discusses what balanced life is and why it is important. It presents the Balanced Life Model and defines the key elements to your balanced lifestyle.

The third chapter, *The Internal and External Root Causes of Life Imbalance,* focuses on the human tendency of dealing with surface causes rather than root causes. Real-life case studies illustrate these findings.

In the fourth chapter, *40 Practical Ideas for Developing Your Personal Balanced Life Plan,* you'll find ideas that have been successfully used by people who face tremendous pressures and demands in their work life.

The solution approach discussed will involve changes in values within to address the internal root causes and changes in relationships with the outer world to address the external root causes. Intellectual understanding without action will not result in changes needed to regain balanced life. Action without understanding results in shallow or short-lived change. One won't work without the other.

The fifth chapter, *11 Principles and Practices to Unleash Your Leadership and Creativity,* makes it clear that leadership is an extension of the total you, the analytical you and the feeling you — in other words, the human you.

To be the most effective leader, dare to be the human being you can be. We become the human being we can be by celebrating life in its fullness — by leading a balanced life.

The sixth chapter, *Leadership Behaviors for Tapping Discretionary Efforts,* shows there is enormous untapped potential found in the employees of most organizations. The ability to tap the latent commitment, enthusiasm, and creativity of everyone in an organization is demonstrably the one unifying theme found in the achievements of all great organizations. The manager's behavior plays a key role in tapping this discretionary effort.

The seventh chapter, *People Self: The Total Self's Most Fulfilling Part and the Key to People Skills,* discusses how each of the four selves — Career, People, Actualizing and Leisure — provide fulfillment and enjoyment in life. However, it is the People Self that provides the most satisfaction.

The eighth chapter, *The Balanced Life in Action: Conversations with Successful Individuals,* presents conversations with individuals reflecting upon their life experiences. These individuals have achieved success in their chosen field professionally, and at the same time have managed to make significant strides toward leading a balanced lifestyle.

The ninth chapter, *Balanced Life Lessons from Nature,* relates the need for ecological balance in nature to the need for balanced life in humans. All living things in nature want to grow. If a plant is not growing, it is dead. Just as nature is beautiful in its unpolluted state, so is a human being. There is a natural radiance from within on the face of a person enjoying inner harmony.

The tenth chapter, *Balanced Life Checkup,* presents an exercise for a self check-up. The exercise is designed to help you identify the areas of your life where some attention might be helpful.

Whenever I go to a management development seminar or read an article on personal development, I say to myself, "As long as I can pick up one or two good ideas, it will be well worth my time." And I assure you that you will find good ideas every time you open this book.

A Personal Note
From Madan Birla and Dr. Cecilia Miller Marshall

One day in 1979, I found myself standing in my physician's office saying, "Lately I have not been as effective at work as I used to be, especially dealing with people. I am not listening well and find myself upset over things of little or no consequence. And physically I feel drained when I get home."

He told me it was all normal, considering my increasing responsibilities at work, but prescribed some tranquilizers and had me undergo a thorough physical.

The physical showed I had a "pre-ulcer condition," which meant another drug prescription to treat that. On the drive home, however, I kept telling myself, "I'm not going to get dependent on tranquilizers and stomach pills. I don't even like taking many aspirins."

So I began extensive research into the root causes for my emotional and physical distress. Seemingly, I should have been on top of the world. In 10 years at RCA, I had earned three promotions and moved into management. I owned a fine home in a nice suburb with a big yard and two cars in the driveway. I had achieved affluence and success, and had a loving wife and two healthy children.

Over time, however, it became clear to me that the primary cause for the symptoms of stress I was experiencing was that I was trying to do more and more in less and less time. As a result, my life was out of balance. At ever increasing cost to my personal life, work was consuming most of my time and energy.

After moving to Memphis to join Federal Express, I continued my search for solutions to balanced-life issues. This research led me to complete a master's degree in counseling. After presenting a paper called *Managerial Productivity and Life Balance* at the American Counseling Association's annual conference, I sent a copy to Mr. Frederick Smith, Chairman and Chief Executive Officer of Federal Express.

He met with me and suggested I develop and teach a seminar based on the paper for Federal Express managers. As a result, over the past six years I have conducted the two day Leadership and Balanced Life seminar at Federal Express, Rhodes College and the University of Memphis.

This book is based on the concepts from the seminar and personal interviews. The names and identifying information in case studies and interviews have been changed, except in cases where permission was granted.

— **Madan Birla**
Author

• • •

I chose to participate in this project, not because I have achieved the perfect balance in my life, but because I believe the quest is so important. In my personal and professional experiences, I see balanced-life concerns everywhere.

Many families who seek therapy are not suffering deeply rooted psychological problems. They are simply suffering from the physical and emotional exhaustion that comes from trying to do too many things at once.

I am grateful to friends, family, clients and colleagues who have shared with me their own quests for a balanced life. Whenever the experiences of others are reported in this book, all details and identifying information have been significantly altered in order to preserve privacy and confidentiality. Any resemblance of the stories to actual individuals is purely coincidental.

It is quite likely, however, that the stories you read will sound quite familiar — because the search for a satisfying life is something we all have in common!

— **Dr. Cecilia Miller Marshall**
Co-author

Balanced Life
and Leadership Excellence

The Unbalanced Life

Balanced Life Concerns Are Not Unique to You

A person has two things to aim at in life: First, to get what you want, and after that to enjoy it. Only the wisest of people achieve the second.

— Logan Pearsall Smith

MAYBE YOU HAVE HEARD COMMENTS like the ones below. Maybe you have found yourself saying things like this. Maybe you still are.

Bill — 42-year-old vice president: With the increased responsibility and workload, I just don't seem to have any time and energy left to do the things I want to do with my family and friends.

Joan — 31-year-old editor: Sure, it's good that I have just been made editor of a 60,000 circulation magazine, but what I really want to do is start a family.

Susan — 39-year-old attorney: When I got pregnant with our second child, I said it was time to drop out for a while. I did, and in fact have recently had child number three. But the longer I stay away from work, the more I miss the stimulation and challenge, not to mention the money. I continually worry about my re-entry and how I will balance all aspects of my life, but I've got to do something.

Balanced Life Concerns are Everywhere

In the Workplace: Recent news articles on changes in the work force indicate that company attitudes toward family life and family-oriented benefits (child care, family leave, scheduling) are

influencing career decisions as much as salary, prestige and location.

A recent top graduate in international business began his
job interviews, not with discussions of opportunities for
advancement, but with questions about how the companies
promoted a well-balanced personal lifestyle.

A senior systems analyst at a small company has passed up
numerous chances to move to larger companies at higher
salaries because of the peace of mind he has as a single parent knowing his two children are nearby in the company
child care center.

*Workers who
neglect their per-
sonal and family
concerns often
become less pro-
ductive at work —
no matter how
many hours they
spend there.*

Statistics indicate that the very
nature of the work force continues to
change in ways that make balanced life
concerns more critical. In the next few
years, two-thirds of new entrants into the
work force will be women. Two-thirds of
those women expect to become pregnant
during their working years, and 40 percent expect to become responsible for
aging parents.

Neither the "fast track" nor the
"Mommy track" will meet these changing
needs adequately. The traditional "fast
track" demands long days, short week-
ends and subjugation of personal and family life to corporate interests. The "Mommy track," described by researcher Felice Schwartz
in 1989, defines a limited work role for those persons who wish to
parent while continuing to work.

Neither track acknowledges certain realities:
• Single working parents are often both "Mommy" and "Daddy."
• Many significant contributions to the workplace will be lost by
relegating family-oriented workers to the restricted role of the
"Mommy track."
• Workers who neglect their personal and family concerns often

become less productive at work — no matter how many hours they spend there.

In the Media: Television and magazine ads, long recognized as windows on our culture, are reflecting balanced-life concerns. A recent magazine ad for IBM featured the headline:

The first computer to understand you don't just have a job. You have a life.

The ad goes on to identify "trying to strike a better balance between the work you do and the life you lead" as the newest national pastime!

Faith Popcorn's best-seller, *The Popcorn Report*, describes trends in the culture that will influence marketing over the next decade. Terms such as "cocooning," "cashing out" and "corporate soul" reflect people's increasing needs for privacy, growing disenchantment with the culture of sushi and BMWs and rising concerns over a corporation's mission in society, as well as its profit-and-loss statement.

New businesses, unheard of only a few years ago, are providing services such as shopping, bill paying, closet organizing, and gift buying so that people can have a little time left at the end of the day.

Among Teenagers: A recent survey conducted by the Bedford Kent Youth Group indicated that quality-of-life concerns — family, friends, community, time to relax, and time to do good — are more important to teenagers than fast fortunes. The same survey indicated that family relationships are rated by teenagers as very important.

Among Women: *Time* magazine reported in 1989 that 73 percent of women surveyed complained of too little leisure activity (as did 51 percent of men) and that helping women balance work and family was identified as the most important goal of the women's movement today. Concerns with helping women achieve corporate success have been replaced by concerns with helping them to achieve life success and to have the time to enjoy it!

Feminist Gloria Steinem's newest book turns to the journey within. She describes her personal search for self-worth and reveals that being admired, successful, and a nationally known leader did not guarantee a feeling of personal well-being.

She does not, however, advocate a return to the Mom-at-home and Dad-at-work solution of the Fifties. Ms. Steinem acknowledges that personal growth and relationships work together with social and political change and professional achievement to create a climate in which people of both genders can be successful and make a contribution to the world.

Meditations For Women Who Do Too Much, by Anne Wilson Schaef, provides 365 days worth of messages for women whose life has gotten somehow out of hand. The sheer number of women represented through the quotes and life experiences is staggering. The theme for February 5 is "exhaustion." It begins with the amusing quote from Charlotte Linton:

> *Whatever women do they must do twice as well as men to be thought half as good. Luckily, this is not difficult.*

In trying to "do it all," women have indeed become exhausted. Exhaustion is a very real signal that one's life is out of balance.

Among Men: The media also reflect changing roles and needs of men. In November 1989, *Esquire* magazine produced a handbook about child-rearing! Full-page ads show fathers as well as mothers holding diapered infants. The uninvolved father in a business suit is no longer the primary role model upon which major advertising campaigns are built.

In 1990, psychologist Marvin Kinder traded his Jaguar for a second-hand Acura and wrote a book about his and his clients' experiences in choosing simpler, more balanced lifestyles. In addition to describing others who, like himself, made major and dramatic changes, he also discusses the advantages of less obvious changes such as reaching professional plateaus.

Instead of viewing a slowing of upward mobility as an indicator of professional deterioration, he encourages people to use it as an opportunity. Plateaus can be turned into periods of tremendous growth by using the time and energy for rest and rejuvenation, polishing neglected skills, developing new relationships, re-evaluating goals and values, and planning for long-term growth and development.

If So Many of Us So Strongly Feel the Need for Leading a Balanced Life — Then Why Aren't More of Us Achieving It?

We live in a country of vast resources and varied opportunities. Our forefathers (and mothers) came from all over the world to the United States seeking freedom, but we, their descendants, seem to have lost our sense of freedom. We have become slaves to our work, our expectations, our possessions, our mortgage payments. We are intelligent, capable, and sensitive people. Why can we not seem to gain control over our own lives?

Plateaus can be turned into periods of tremendous growth by using the time and energy for long-term growth and development.

1. We do not know how.

We want to have a balanced and healthy lifestyle, but we do not know how because we are not born with the secret of how to live. The modern lifestyle requires skills that our parents and even some of our mentors did not have or need to have. To develop balanced-life skills requires that we be willing to be patient, to experiment, and to make a commitment to continuously update our skills and information.

2. We procrastinate.

We mean to get back to these balanced-life concerns but we have bills to pay, things to do, career opportunities to seize, planes to catch, and activities to pursue. Before we know it another year has passed. We avoid dealing with balanced-life issues directly, but they never quite seem to go away.

3. **We employ unhealthy substances and strategies to manage the stress caused by an unbalanced lifestyle.**

• **Chemicals:** *I need a drink!*

In the United States, the top two prescription drugs are not antibiotics or birth-control pills. They are two different types of tranquilizers. Although tranquilizers and other prescription drugs have many appropriate, helpful and healthful uses, they may become simply another means of avoiding the balanced-life issues that created the stress in the first place. Consider Bill's story:

> Bill was a 30-year-old minister with a wife in graduate school, a new baby and the relentlessly busy Christmas season approaching. He had been unable to shake a chronic cough and cold, and went to his physician for medication to get him back on his feet so he could resume his duties. Before the physical exam, the physician took a detailed life history, including current health habits, responsibilities and stresses.
>
> Instead of the expected prescription for strong antibiotics, Bill received advice on a change in diet, an exercise plan and strategies for stress management. Accompanied by a mild cough medicine, this "prescription" made a difference, not only in Bill's cough but also in his life!

Every day is valuable for itself and not just as a means to tomorrow's achievements. Life has to be lived today.

• **Living in the future:** *Everything will be fine just as soon as I ... get the promotion, build the house, etc.*

The problem with this coping strategy is that the future, by definition, never arrives. The new job, house, boat or spouse rarely brings the longed-for satisfaction, and the race goes on. It is good to have goals, but always looking to the future stops us from living in the present. One important lesson often learned by those facing serious illness is that every day is valuable for itself and not just as a means to tomorrow's achievements. Life has to be lived today.

- **Projection:** *I'm doing it for them.*

We know our life is out of balance, but we rationalize that we are providing more material things for our families. If we took time to ask our children and spouse what they really want, we might be surprised at the answers.

Consider the responses of a group of business executives asked to give a two-minute talk about themselves. The exercise was an "ice breaker" speech at the meeting of a civic club. The executives talked about happy memories of childhood, fishing trips with Dad, family camping trips, summer at the beach, school plays, piano recitals.

No one talked about the kind of clothes they wore, the kind of house they lived in, the expensive toys they played with or the make and model of the family car. When asked to tell about who they were, the executives talked about shared experiences and happy memories of times when parents gave of themselves.

- **Externalizing:** *I need a new job.*

Changing jobs, locations, cars or houses may be helpful if it is the sincere desire for the new job, location, car or house that motivates the change. Change, however, may also be used to avoid problems that need to be resolved. Consider Mark's story:

Mark was telling a friend over lunch about his recent physical. The doctor had suggested that Mark change jobs to reduce stress and the resulting high-blood pressure.

The friend remarked, "Maybe it will help, and maybe it will not. Even in the new job, you are going to take Mark wherever you go." Ultimately, Mark decided to change the job. At last report, however, his family did not like the move, and he is thinking of moving again.

- **Compensating:** *What I really need is a new ... house, car, boat, etc.*

We feel that something is missing but instead of finding out which one of our balanced-life needs is going unmet, we listen to the media and try to fill the empty space with increased material consumption: designer clothes, gourmet food, sophisticated sound equipment, faster cars, etc. Such things give temporary relief from the symptoms, but the real problem keeps eating at the stomach lining.

- **Fatalism:** *I guess that's the price for success.*

The day after Jack got the big promotion he had sought so frantically for three years, his wife decided to file for divorce. Jack was disappointed, but shrugged it off, saying, "I guess that's the price of success." Instead of looking within and coming to terms with his unbalanced life, he simply resigned himself to the easy excuse of a false reality.

- **Disengagement:** *There's nothing I can do.*

Disengagement is a frequent consequence of workers finding themselves in a professional plateau or other situation in which promotion, salary increase or job growth seems impossible. To compensate for the lack of anticipated rewards and to balance the scale, the amount of effort expended is simply reduced. The worker resigns without actually quitting the job. She or he simply reduces effort, involvement and creativity.

> Dana resigned from her job without leaving the office! A regular cycle of three-year promotions came to an end after she had risen to a position in which her immediate superior was a young person unlikely to leave or retire within the near future. So Dana simply maintained the status quo and resisted any new or creative ideas that demanded more effort. The result was that her need to be challenged at work was unmet, and she began to experience a feeling of diminished success off the job as well.

- **Avoidance:** *I just need to finish one more project and then I'll relax.*

The above quote could easily be made by a confirmed workaholic the day before the massive heart attack signals that he or she has finished too many projects already. The different parts of the total self send signals through the body, mind and spirit when life gets out of balance: the nagging headaches, backaches, restlessness; the feeling that something's missing but you can't put your finger on it.

These experiences are trying to tell us, "Hey! Something's out of balance!" — much as the buzzer on an automatic washing machine signals loudly that the load has become unbalanced and needs attention. If we responded as quickly to the signals of our body and mind as we do to the buzzing of the washing machine, balanced-life issues would be resolved much more easily.

Other people also send us signals, if only we will listen. How many times in the past week have you put off your child, spouse, parent or friend with the excuse of "Just as soon as I finish this."

- **Passivity:** *It's out of my control.*

Another common coping mechanism is to play the passive or victim role and blame a lack of balanced life on a supervisor who expects too much, the length of the "to do" list at home, non-supportive spouse, demanding children, etc.

Phrases such as "What can I do?" or "It's out of my control," or "I've tried everything," indicate passivity. This rationalization may bring temporary relief from trying to solve the problem, but the pressure continues to build.

- **Analyzing, intellectualizing:** *I/you should be happy.*

Statements regarding how another person "should" feel are often made by someone who hasn't a clue as to how she or he (or anyone else) is actually feeling! A focus on logical and concrete events ignores the emotional, personal, and spiritual components of life. The media and society reinforce this approach by implying, "If you have everything, you should be happy."

> *If we responded as quickly to the signals of our body and mind as we do to the buzzing of the washing machine, balanced-life issues would be resolved much more easily.*

Dick, a very successful business executive, became distraught upon finding out that his wife had become an alcoholic. "I just don't understand," he said. "I make good money. We live in a beautiful house, drive imported cars, and have a nice portfolio."

In Dick's mind, with all these things, there was no excuse for Marsha to be depressed and resort to alcohol. He had ignored the importance of his wife's definition of success, which included emotional, relational and spiritual well-being, as well as material affluence.

What is the Healthy Way to Deal with Balanced-Life Issues?

The power to lead a balanced lifestyle is within each one of us. Before we can tap that power, we have to give up the victim role and take responsibility for our lives. We have to reclaim our lives from the habits, expectations, roles, people and situations that keep us frustrated and unfulfilled. Where we are today in our lives is a summation of all the countless choices — big and small — that we have made. Where we will be in 10 years begins with the choices we make today. When we truly understand and accept this responsibility, then we are on our way to a successful life journey.

Each one of us is unique in aspirations, achievements, frustrations and environments. There cannot be one solution that will apply to all situations. If someone gives you a "canned" or ready-made formula for balanced life, be very cautious.

The process presented here for addressing and managing balanced-life issues is one that should help you develop solutions that fit the uniqueness of your environment. As you grow and your life changes, new approaches will be required to help keep your life in balance.

The Balanced Life Four-Step Process:

1. **Visualizing the balanced, healthy state, and taking charge of your life balance.**

2. **Identifying the root causes of imbalance in your life — the internal as well as the external root causes.**

3. **Developing a personal action plan to address the root causes identified in Step 2.**

4. **Taking action to implement the plan. Got to do it!**

Is it easy to lead a balanced life in this fast-paced and competitive world?

No!

Is it possible?

Yes!

Do you have the resources to make it happen?

Yes!

Why should you bother now?

There is no dress rehearsal in this life. We do not get a second chance. We have to live and enjoy the life as we go along.

If we don't stop and take charge now, then we run the risk of drifting into a lifestyle and not realizing until it is too late that this is not the kind of life we wanted at all.

Visualizing the Balanced Healthy State and Balanced Life Four-Step Process

What is Balanced Life and Why is It Important?

There is more to life than increasing its speed.
— Mahatma Gandhi

WHAT ARE WE AFTER IN LIFE? This is the first question asked of business and professional leaders in the Leadership and Balanced Life seminar conducted by the author. Responses of participants usually reflect themes of happiness, success, sense-of-contribution, love, making money, financial security, and self-fulfillment.

Discussion on the follow-up question ("Why do you want happiness, success, money ...") frequently generates the response: "Because it makes me feel good about myself." This discussion is followed by the request that participants write down the things, activities, and accomplishments that have made them feel good about themselves within the past year.

Before reading further, complete the exercise yourself: *Write down the experiences, activities and accomplishments that have made you feel good within the past year.* (Don't cheat and skip ahead to the next section. This is important!)

Now, compare your responses to those of other business and professional leaders who have completed this exercise. (The notations following each response will be explained later in the chapter.)

Cecilia —Psychologist in private practice:
1. Working with increasing number of child/family clients in my practice (C/A)
2. Sewing French dresses for my daughters (P)

3. Reading some good books (L)
4. Sharing with my husband new ideas he gained during his study (P/A)
5. Getting reconnected with old and new friends at Rhodes Forum (P)
6. Church activities (A)

Madan — Federal Express Executive:
1. Playing tennis twice a week (L)
2. Evening walks with wife (P)
3. Attending my daughter's softball games (P)
4. Son graduating from school in top 10 percent of his class (P)
5. Sunday School activities (A)
6. Assuming more responsibility at work (C)

David — Sonoco Products:
1. Introduced a new quality-improvement program at work (C)
2. Successfully reduced our plant's budget by $25,000 (C)
3. Visited South Carolina, Louisiana, Florida for pleasure (L)
4. Had the best Christmas with my family in years (P)
5. Saw my sister after a two-year absence (P)
6. More involved with the local food bank and organ transplant center (A)

Susan — Fogelman Executive Center at University of Memphis:
1. Recognition from employer for hard work done on a major project (C)
2. Love and support from family and friends (P)
3. Inner strength, which carried me through some rough spots (A)
4. Faith in God (A)
5. Renovation of my new (older) home (L)

Ron — Dow Corning Wright:
1. Solving a difficult situation at work (C)
2. Relating well with my daughters and wife (P)
3. Helping my children with homework (P)
4. Having a good relationship with church friends (P)

5. Having extra income to use for travel (L)
6. Hearing a good sermon (A)

Debbie — Peabody Hotel:
1. Trip to Nashville with husband and kids (P/L)
2. Exceeded my own sales goals at work (C)
3. Planned several events at work that went very well — happy clients (C)
4. Started aerobics classes in June and kept with it (L)
5. Lost weight, so look a little better (L/A)
6. Managed to live through another X-mas season both professionally and personally without a nervous breakdown (A)

Bill — South Central Bell:
1. Good friends — friendship with some have gotten stronger. I help them and they help me (P)
2. Successful completion of several major projects at work (C)
3. Received good evaluation, pay raise and bonus (C)
4. Relationship with my girlfriend (P)
5. Playing in several concerts. I enjoy playing the saxophone (L)
6. Growing relationship with God (A)

Jonathan — National Safety Associates:
1. Market development in Germany (C)
2. Helping daughter in college situation (P)
3. Outreach to rest of the company (C)
4. Was able to re-kindle leisure pursuits (L)
5. Meeting financial goals (C)

Why did people write these things down? Why did you answer as you did?

People feel good when a need is satisfied. When we are thirsty, drinking cold water feels good — satisfaction of a physical need. The same is true of psychological needs.

The preceding responses show that the psychological self is multi-dimensional, that a multitude of things/experiences are important to satisfying our psychological needs. It is not a coincidence that each list contains items that address one or more of the following needs: (C) career; (P) people; (A) actualization; (L) leisure.

This is true despite the fact that respondents were quite dissimilar in age, occupation, income and professional/business specialty. People feel fulfilled when important human needs are satisfied.

NEEDS	SOURCES OF SATISFACTION	SPECIFIC REWARDS (need satisfiers)
Recognition/esteem: "I want to be somebody."	CAREER	Power, social status, recognition, leadership opportunities, money.
Love, belonging: "I want to be somebody to somebody."	PEOPLE	Mutual support, attention, affection, sexuality and sensuality, group membership, shared experiences, communication.
Identity, self-respect: "I want to be somebody to myself."	ACTUALIZATION	Being in touch with the physical, emotional, mental and spiritual environment; reaching goals we set for ourselves; sense of meaning and coherence in life.
Physical, relaxation: "I want a break from the pressures of being/ becoming somebody."	LEISURE	Activities chosen "just for fun" and not for making a living; recharging one's batteries.

What this exercise tells us is that we need to examine our life experiences to see for ourselves what leads to fulfillment/happiness and what leads to conflict/stress. We don't have to accept blindly the wisdom of how-to books or psychologists. We have the raw material: life experiences. What we need is time for reflection and introspection.

We need to examine our life experiences to see for ourselves what leads to fulfillment/happiness and what leads to conflict/stress. We don't have to accept blindly the wisdom of how-to books or psychologists.

Interestingly enough, the real-life observations reflected in the author's surveys are consistent with the findings of well-known psychologists, such as Abraham Maslow, Carl Rogers and William Glasser. These researchers have devoted much of their study to the functioning of healthy individuals, identifying ways to help "normal" individuals function more effectively.

Physical/Relaxation Needs

Abraham Maslow studied healthy people in the belief that healthy people can teach others about higher levels of human awareness and ways to achieve them.

He described five primary sets of needs that motivate human behavior: physiological, safety/security, love and belongingness, esteem, and self-actualization. These needs are arranged in a hierarchical fashion, because the basic survival needs must be satisfied before others can be addressed.

The basic physiological needs are food, water, air, and shelter. Although leisure, physical exercise and relaxation were not included in Maslow's original list, physical well-being is clearly indicated as an important human need.

Physical and relaxation needs are often relegated to the "back burner" in modern society until the body clearly signals its distress through a heart attack or ulcer. Suddenly, at that point, making time for exercise becomes a life-giving necessity rather than a low-priority frill.

Taking care of our bodies through nutrition, exercise, rest and relaxation enables us to address our needs for recognition, belonging and identity more effectively.

Love/Belonging Needs

According to William Glasser, the difference between psychologically healthy people and others is based on whether or not an individual has a "success identity" or a "failure identity." This identity is developed through interaction with others as others provide feedback.

An integral part of this interpersonal transaction is the need to love and be loved — "I am somebody *to* somebody." People who are successful at motivating others — managers, teachers, coaches, parents — have been applying these principles successfully for years.

Glasser's concept of "success identity" is important to the development of recognition and esteem needs as well.

Recognition/Esteem Needs

Esteem needs consist of the desires for reputation and respect from others. Psychologist Carl Rogers uses the term "unconditional positive regard" to describe the experience of being valued for what one is, rather than for what one should be or ought to be; being valued for being as well as for doing; being recognized for one's strengths rather than for one's weaknesses.

Human beings of all ages need such experiences if they are to realize their potentials and develop their talents and abilities. Successful leaders and managers know this and use this skill in helping their employees identify and utilize their strengths, rather than berating them for their failures.

Esteem and respect from others provide a foundation for self-esteem and self-respect, and point the way toward attainment of the highest level of human awareness: self-actualization.

Self-Actualization

Carl Rogers also writes of the drive to achieve psychological maturity, which he believed to be deeply rooted in human nature. Important questions in personal growth are "How can I become what I deeply wish to become?" and "How can I get behind my facades and become myself?"

These questions are also contained in Maslow's concept of self-actualization, which includes a person's desire to reach his or her potential in a multi-dimensional way: personal, social, occupational, physical, and spiritual.

The experience of self-actualization is more than just achieving a singular personal, corporate or financial goal. It is the experience of feeling that one is exercising a unique and precious combination of skills and abilities; that one is fulfilling a special purpose of making a special contribution; and that one's life is connected to a larger sense of purpose or meaning.

Spiritual development, a central part of self-actualization, is defined by people in many ways. Although the term "spiritual" is often used by people with formal religious affiliation, it is a universal human experience.

Jean Grasso Fitzpatrick defines the word spiritual as "an awareness of our sacred connection with all of life," and spiritual nurture as "the opportunity to share with our children something more enduring than the hope of success or even happiness." If we are to have this "something" to share with children or others whom we care about, we must take the time to develop or nurture it within ourselves.

Most 2-year-olds know intuitively how to focus attention. When speaking to a distracted adult, they will often take your face between their hands and turn it toward theirs, thereby gaining your undivided attention. Five minutes of such undivided attention is worth more than hours of half-hearted inattention, whether we are giving it to ourselves or to others.

Anne Wilson Schaef acknowledged this important reality in writing her book, *Meditations for Women Who Do Too Much*. Each day's meditation is less than a page in length, and most take less than

> *Self-actualization is more than just achieving a singular personal, corporate or financial goal. It is the experience of feeling ... that one's life is connected to a larger sense of purpose or meaning.*

a minute to read. Using such a resource daily, only five minutes per day, a person could add 30 hours of spiritual nurture to each year of his or her life.

Theologian Frederick Buechner puts the matter succinctly:

Pay attention to your life.

If we are to pay attention to our lives, we must not be paying attention to half a dozen other things as well. Clearing out the mind for even a few moments each day is a good beginning for the life-long process of spiritual development and self-actualization.

The Balanced Life Model

The Balanced Life Model incorporates the fundamental psychological concepts of human needs as motivators, the presence of an innate drive toward psychological maturity, and the importance of identity for psychological health and personal success.

This model represents the integration of the author's work in management and leadership training with the basic psychological principles described above. It is a multi-dimensional model that can be illustrated graphically:

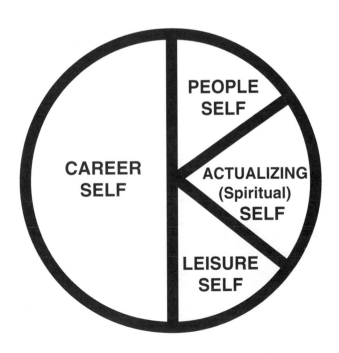

The Balanced Life Model has eight key characteristics. The following case studies show how the model operates in real-life situations.

1.   The Total Self Must be Regarded Not As a Collection of Isolated Components, but As One Integrated Whole

Consider Bill's story. He joined his division two years before as a manager of planning, is good at what he does and had always been a positive leader. Recently, however, he had become openly critical of management and very negative in general. A colleague noticed the change and approached Bill about it.

COLLEAGUE: Bill, is there something I can help you with? You have not been your positive self lately.

BILL: You're right. When I joined the department two years ago, I was promised that I would be reporting to the Vice President — my boss's boss. Now, when I ask for that, I am told that no such promise was made.

COLLEAGUE: It is obvious that this is bothering you very much. If the reporting level is that important to you, then maybe you need to change jobs. This may mean moving, since other industries in your field are out of state.

BILL: I don't want to move. I like the neighborhood we live in and the church we attend. We all like living only an hour away from both my parents and my wife's parents. I enjoy coaching the boys' soccer team and playing golf without having to spend a fortune doing it. I also like the people in my department and the peers I work with.

COLLEAGUE: The only thing you really don't like about your life is the reporting level in the organization, and to change that you may have to sacrifice other things you like.

BILL: That's a different way to look at the situation.

COLLEAGUE (some time later): The holistic look at the situation made Bill think, and I noticed a change in him, back to being a positive leader.

DISCUSSION: When making career decisions, the tendency is to look at career in isolation from other aspects of life. Decisions and choices made in this way are not the optimum choices in terms of overall life fulfillment. As Bill's situation illustrates, such a narrow decision-making focus may also be destructive to a career as well!

REFLECTION: Take a moment to look at your whole life — the big picture. In each of the four areas (Career, People, Actualizing, and Leisure) write down what is satisfying to you.

2. Expansion in One Component Cannot Compensate for a Missing Component

Last week Mark finally got the position he had been working for: Vice President of Sales. The same week, his wife asked him for a divorce.

Mark was devastated and said to his friends, "I just want one more chance to prove that I can be a good husband and father. I'll change jobs. I'll change towns."

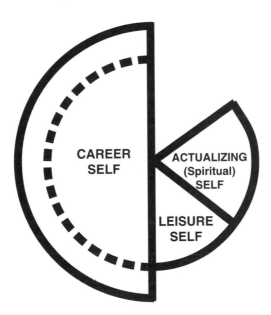

DISCUSSION: Mark had let himself become "married to the job" and did not have any time for his wife. His situation illustrates the fact that career advancements are satisfying and fulfilling to the

Career Self but cannot compensate for fulfillment of the People Self. It took a tragic event to bring this to Mark's attention!

REFLECTION: Look at your calendar. How much time is devoted to the important people/relationships in your life?

3. Only the Individual Can Define for Himself or Herself the Scope and Sources of Fulfillment Within Each of the Four Components of the Balanced Life Circle

A month after attending the Leadership and Balanced Life seminar, Jane phoned the leader to say she had some good news to announce: "I just called to let you know that I declined a promotion!"

By using the Balanced Life Model to evaluate the total life impact of accepting versus not accepting the promotion, Jane came to the conclusion that at this point in time she was happier without the added pressure. The job involved 50 percent travel. With two pre-teen daughters, Jane did not wish to be away from home that much. Although everyone in her department was pressuring her to take the job, she felt happy and satisfied in declining it at this time.

DISCUSSION: Jane did not fall into the trap of allowing other people to define her life needs and sources of satisfaction. Although accepting the promotion might have been a very fruitful decision for another of her colleagues, it was not best for Jane at the time. She used the expanded definition of "success" and the Balanced Life Model to evaluate the impact of a decision in one area of life upon her life as a whole. Not only will she be a happier person, but she will also perform better at work when her whole life is in balance.

REFLECTION: What is an important decision facing you right now? How will that decision impact your life as a whole (Career, People, Actualizing, Leisure).

4. Each Component Has Its Own Joys and Disappointments

Ann was devastated when the doctor told her that "tennis elbow" was acting up and that she should give up playing for a while. She reacted as though she'd been told she had only a few months to live. Her children remarked that she looked as if she'd just lost her best friend.

Ann has been frustrated for several years at her under-stimulating job and has also felt less needed at home as her two children entered their pre-teen years. So tennis had become her avenue for accomplishment and achievement. She devoted herself diligently to the game and became quite good at it.

She became so good, in fact, that she neglected other areas of her life. She literally lived all week for her weekend matches, and her mood for the week was usually determined by her "score" of the previous weekend. In her own eyes, Ann's tennis score reflected the sum total of her self worth.

Twenty-eight-year-old Dan was devastated when the mental-health center to which he had devoted the past five years of his life suddenly lost its funding and began laying off employees. His work had been his source of career development, leisure time activity, personal friendship and self-esteem. He socialized, worked and played with co-workers, and had few interests outside his work and colleagues.

The layoffs threatened not only his own job security but also the close-knit social system to which he belonged. More than his career was at stake here. Dan saw his whole life hanging in the balance of administrative decisions made by others.

DISCUSSION: The Career Self provides joy through challenges and sense of accomplishment but it also provides disappointments. Leisure activities provide relaxation and challenges but also frustrations. The point is that no one part of the self can provide all of life's kicks all of the time. Once we understand that, then we don't put all our eggs in one basket by investing all our time and energy in just one part of the self.

REFLECTION: Close your eyes and imagine for a moment what your life would be like if you had only your career to meet your needs. What would your life be like without leisure, people, or actualization experiences?

5. Each Component is Supportive of the Others in Both Success and Failure

Roger got the big promotion! He immediately called his wife and best friend and announced the date for the celebration. The satisfaction of his business success was multiplied when it was shared with others. How much less satisfying it might have been if there had been no one to call with the good news.

DISCUSSION: It is a well-documented fact that individuals with supportive and understanding relationships are better able to withstand the stresses of the modern-day, fast-paced lifestyle. The recent proliferation of corporate gyms and health programs is not just a reflection of increased health-consciousness. It is also a reflection of the increased productivity that is seen in healthy employees. Good health and good relationships make economic sense as well as personal sense.

The Balanced Life Model is made up of two halves: Career (C) and Personal (PAL). The Personal life is not in conflict with the Career (C) but in fact is very supportive (hence, the letters PAL !) The personal relationships, self-actualization and leisure activities are not in competition with career development, but work together as a supportive unit.

REFLECTION: Have you ever had some good news, phoned a friend and found the line busy? Remember your disappointment and frustration? This experience illustrates the important support role of each part of the Balanced Life Model. Success is more sweet and failure more bearable if there are friends and family members with whom to share it.

6. The Ceiling to One's Personal Happiness is Set by the Component of Lowest Satisfaction

George was eating a delicious Mexican dinner with two colleagues in a beautiful restaurant in downtown San Antonio. He had just made a successful presentation at a prestigious professional conference.

George said, "Guys, I'm in the company of good friends ... having just presented a good paper ... enjoying a nice meal. Why don't I feel so good?"

Further discussion revealed that he was not very happy in his job, and that was stopping him from enjoying the present moment 100 percent.

DISCUSSION: A person may appear very happy in her or his work and leisure activities. If he or she is miserable in the People part of life, however, then the personal rating of overall happiness will not be much above that of the People situation. The same is true of dissatisfaction with Career or Leisure. Like George, a person may be fulfilling Actualization, People and Leisure needs, and still feel unfulfilled because the Career Self is out of balance.

REFLECTION: Stop right now and "live in the moment!" What are the satisfactions you are receiving from your career ... from your people relationships ... from your self-actualization ... your leisure activities?

7. The Components Have to be Taken Apart from Time to Time and Refitted Together

"I can't understand it," muses Catherine, an attorney with a large corporate firm. "My friends can't understand it. Two years ago, I was the original 'party animal.' I could stay up later and go out more nights than anyone I knew, and still turn in a dynamite performance at work. I still enjoy my friends and my work, but all I want to do in the evenings now is curl up with a good book by the fire or have an occasional casual evening with a few close friends. Is something wrong?"

DISCUSSION: The distribution of energy and time to each of the four components of a balanced life has to be changed as we grow older, as life circumstances change and as the world changes. Psychologist Erik Erickson identified specific stages of adult development that are similar to the developmental stages that children experience. Gail Sheehy popularized this notion in her bestseller, *Passages*. Faith Popcorn's recent best-seller, *The Popcorn Report*, identifies social trends, such as "cocooning" and describes their impact on the way people live and the products they buy.

As we grow, our needs change. Self-actualization and spiritual development take greater importance as we grow older than when we were starting our careers. The intensity of relationship needs that are prominent in young adulthood later give way to needs for productivity and then for contribution and mentoring. The task for the individual in each transition is to achieve the new balance. It is an ongoing process.

The whole idea behind developmental changes is that things can never be settled once and for all. Life is a thriller all right, but not one we can solve with one "right" set of clues. Life is not a puzzle with only one correct fit. Getting it right at 30 will not be the same as getting it right at 20. The activities that relieved stress in 1980 may accelerate stress in 1990.

REFLECTION: Compare what gives meaning to your life now with what did so 10 years ago. They are different. Why? Not because you didn't have it "right" 10 years ago, but because you and your world have changed and grown.

8. **Each Component Has Elements of Others, but Cannot Totally Substitute for the Others, as Each Component Provides its Own Unique Fulfillment**
Bill is a successful businessman whose daily routine is coming

home late, eating dinner and retiring to the study with his laptop computer and brief case. In a recent conversation he said, "I love my job. I get a lot of satisfaction and enjoyment. I had my physical last week and the doctor was insisting that I take up a leisure activity. I don't have time for a leisure activity. My wife is also insisting on some activity we can do together."

DISCUSSION: Society in general and corporate life in particular encourage people to define their worth solely in terms of career and material success. Since there is only so much room at the top of the corporate pyramid, this narrow definition leaves us extremely vulnerable, often feeling failed and frustrated. Extra hours spent doing work cannot substitute for the relaxation provided by leisure. Although we develop collegial relationships at work, they are not substitutes for the kind of joy provided by the more intimate family and friendship relationships.

Conclusion

This chapter began with the question: What is a balanced life, and why is it important? A balanced life is a model for living that is based on positive assumptions about human growth and motivation. A balanced life can be visualized as a balanced healthy state in which the individual uses all of his or her skills, takes charge of his or her life and celebrates life in its fullness.

In our own way, each one of us is pursuing happiness. No doubt, career success is one source of happiness. The ambition providing the drive for success is good, but a blindly ambitious person is self-destructive. A person who is never satisfied with his or her success and always keeps pushing is headed for trouble — if not in trouble already!

Here are some important questions to ask yourself:

- Whose happiness are you pursuing? Is it your own defin-ition of success, worth and identity — or someone else's?

- Are you in touch with your own definition of "success identity" — or do you allow your boss, friends, family or the media to define your life for you?

- Does your calendar reflect the life you own, or does it appear to be someone else's?

Periodically, we need to evaluate our beliefs and goals in light of our own life experiences and replace them with more enlight-ened beliefs. By paying attention to our own life experiences, we are validating whether or not our internal measure of success is truly our own or what someone else has "sold" to us.

Life experiences tell us there is no happiness without peace of mind. Happiness is not a result of what happens to us but what hap-pens in us when that harmonious self within is at peace. It is folly to think that peace will come along like a cloud from the heavens. Thoughtful people generate their peace from within.

Being at peace with one's self means being in touch with all dimensions of the self: the changing needs; what makes you ful-filled; the directions you're taking; and, most important, the bal-ance between the Career, People, Actualizing and Leisure aspects of your life.

Once we get in touch with our lives as a whole and expand the definition of success, we begin to lead life differently — a life reflecting more balanced allocation of money, time and energy to the four needs of the Balanced Life Model.

It is liberating to realize that the smaller house is more fulfill-ing than the bigger house if the relationships inside the house are becoming deeper. It is liberating to realize that greater life fulfill-ment is a lifestyle that allows time to engage in leisure and self-actualization activities. It is liberating to realize that doing what you enjoy and experiencing a sense of accomplishment can be as ful-filling as a bigger title.

It is the four components — Career, People, Leisure, and Actualization — when combined, that make us whole.

Inside and Out

The Internal and External Root Causes of Life Imbalance

We can chart our future clearly and wisely only when we know the path which has led to the present.

— Adlai Stevenson

EXTERNAL DEMANDS FROM JOB and career are a reality. However, the demands are rarely as absolute as they seem to be. In the final analysis, each person decides how many hours she or he will give to the job.

The key word here is decides. Although a job or employer may limit the options (For example: Work 16 hours a day if you want a promotion), in the final analysis it is the worker who decides whether or not the promotion is worth the price.

In this chapter we deal with internal and external causes of life imbalance. It is important to recognize how the external demands of our work and environment do affect our choices and the outcomes of our decisions.

It is equally important to recognize how our internal beliefs and thought processes affect how we respond to external pressures and the way in which we perceive what "must" be done. The key to attaining a better life balance is to recognize and manage both internal and external causes of life imbalance.

External Root Causes of Life Imbalance

Causes of life imbalance may be identified as external when they involve material, physical or emotional demands from someone or something outside ourselves:

1.   **Work environment demanding 16-hour days.**

2. Dual career/single parenting demands — not enough hours in the day.

3. Work at home not evenly shared — gender-role demands

4. Pressure from family, society, media to succeed.

5. Lack of proper training in the use of delegation, prioritizing and time management.

6. Lack of training in the Balanced Life Model for decision making.

1. Work environment demanding 16-hour days

Take your basic 24-hour day, subtract 16 hours for work, and you are left with exactly 8 hours in which to get 6-8 hours sleep, eat three meals, bathe and dress, maintain your home and spend "quality time" with your spouse and/or children. Any third-grade math student can tell you that the numbers simply don't add up!

The obvious solution to this little mathematical dilemma is simple. Either find another planet that has 48-hour days or find a job that demands fewer hours. For many workers, finding a planet with 48-hour days would be easier than coming to grips with the painful reality of their own work schedules.

Where does the 16-hour day come from? In some cases it comes from a boss or manager who puts in long days and expects the same from employees. These individuals typically measure their own success solely in terms of earnings or corporate status and allocate their time accordingly.

This definition of success is imposed on employees and co-workers. Taking time for self, leisure and relationships may be perceived as an act of corporate treason!

Long days are also common in the "helping" professions: teaching, social services, counseling, ministry, medicine, etc. In these fields, professionals encounter human needs on a daily basis. Because the need is often greater than the resources available, the temptation to spend extra time or to do "just one more thing" is almost overwhelming.

Where does a teacher draw the line when many of her students will not pass without after-school tutoring? How does the
Human Resources Director decide to call it a day when a distraught
employee presents himself at two minutes before quitting time.
How does a physician get any rest when her elderly patients refuse
to acknowledge her day off because, they insist, "Nobody else can
take care of me the way you do."

Corporate greed is not the only cause of the 16-hour day.
Reasonable requests from reasonable people can multiply into a 16-
hour day just as easily as unreasonable requests from overly ambitious bosses.

A more subtle and insidious source of the 16-hour day is cultural expectation. The executive who is seen mowing his lawn or
the physician who volunteers to be P.T.A. president is likely to
become suspect. Executives and professionals are just somehow
"supposed" to be at the office from 8 to 5 (or 6, or 8 or 10!). Cultural
stereotypes abound, encouraging overwork at the office and inattention to life balance.

The author and co-author represent both the corporate and
human-services fields. It is our experience that the 16-hour day can
be created just as easily in one setting as another.

The effects of putting in these days are remarkably similar
across professions. Spouses and children come to feel "worth less"
than the office. Professional contributions grow stale. Subtle health
problems begin to crop up. The 16-hour day does not come cheap.
It exacts a steep toll.

2. Dual career/single parenting demands — not enough hours in the day.

For many of us, our mothers and fathers did not prepare us for
the adult world in which we now find ourselves. It was not that
they were intentionally neglectful. They simply could not train us
for something they never experienced.

Fathers who fulfilled the traditional "provider" role were not
expected also to be adept at carpooling, communicating and cooking. Mothers who were full-time homemakers did not have to "steal
time" from work to attend the kindergarten play.

Instead of changing or modifying the roles we saw in our parents, most of us have simply added or multiplied roles. Unfortunately, adding roles and responsibilities does not add any more hours to the day. We work hard and we work "smart." Still, we often feel unsuccessful ... frustrated ... resentful ... overworked.

Amanda and Neal:

Amanda and Neal put every minute of their time to use. Their friends marveled at how productive they were. They both worked full-time during the week and made time to help their children with homework and after-school activities. As there was no time for housework during the week, Amanda and Neal used their weekends to cook ahead for the coming week and to do laundry and housework. Their job responsibilities were fulfilled capably; their house was clean; their meals were nutritious; and their children received plenty of "quality time." Amanda and Neal were exhausted! They couldn't understand why they often felt incomplete and had no time for each other.

> *Instead of changing or modifying the roles we saw in our parents, most of us have simply added or multiplied roles.*

An interesting thing happens (besides exhaustion) when we try to execute multiple roles. While the opportunities for success are multiplied, so are the opportunities for failure. The working parent has the opportunity to be successful in career, parenting, homemaking, time management and leadership. He or she also has opportunities to fail at each of these tasks. It is very tempting to focus only on the failures!

Guilt and frustrated expectations seem to fall especially heavily on working women. Modern dads can change a few diapers, run carpool occasionally, and in just a few hours per week can actually *exceed* the role models with which they grew up! Women who were reared by full-time homemakers can devote 40-50 hours per week to their children and not even *meet* the expectations with which they were reared.

In these situations, it is not only the actual physical and mental demands of our roles, but also our perceptions of what constitutes success and failure that is relevant. What we perceive to be necessary determines how many tasks we take on and how much success or failure we feel at the end of the day.

No working parent (male or female) can get everything done alone. Those who try are chronically frustrated and often bitter. Those who survive learn three important skills:

• Expecting and receiving help from family, friends and paid workers
• Delegating authority
• Setting priorities

These skills are important to any worker or parent. They are the essence of survival for those of us who work and parent.

3. Work at home not evenly shared — gender-role demands

During the height of the post-World War II "baby boom," a father could change a few diapers, attend the school play and grill the occasional weekend steak — and he had pretty well fulfilled his family responsibilities. Balanced life consisted of making time to play golf on weekends, read *The Wall Street Journal*, and take the spouse out to dinner. During this same period, women performed most of the homemaking responsibilities and had few if any personal or cultural pressures for career accomplishments outside the home. Gender roles were clear and responsibilities were divided accordingly.

Today, such clear and simple division of cultural roles and responsibilities exists in only a small minority of American families. Economic and social changes have been so dramatic that the modern family is hard-pressed to catch up in terms of developing viable family roles and equitable divisions of labor.

Division of labor at home continues to be a problem in even the most progressive and "liberated" of households. Studies of two-career families indicate that women continue to perform more than half of all household and child-rearing tasks regardless of the financial or professional status of the parents.

This situation creates problems for both sexes. Men who are actively involved in home and child care may do twice as much as their professional peers, but only half as much as their spouses would like! The dilemma for women is often that of competing professionally with men who are able to use their after-work hours for professional reading and "power golf" rather than laundry, meal-preparation and carpooling.

The tasks that are associated with the female-role stereotype — cooking, cleaning, shopping, nurturing, child care, etc. — cannot be ignored. They are necessities of life. They can also become a bitter battleground between spouses. The time spent arguing over whose job it is to do the laundry could be better spent in devising creative solutions for getting it finished. Consider the following:

SALLY: When my first husband and I divorced, I taught my daughter to do laundry. Now that I am remarried, we continue to be responsible for our own laundry, and my husband does his also.

MEG: During times when I am unusually busy at work, we eat out. The kids love it, and I save not only meal-preparation time but grocery-shopping, planning and clean-up time.

DAVE: Our children each cook dinner one night per week — even the 9-year-old. Not all our meals would make the cover of *Good Housekeeping*, but I have more quality time with my children in the evening, and they are learning independence as well as cooking skills.

Test your own creativity with this exercise: In one minute, list all possible methods of feeding a family of four an evening meal five nights per week.

If you came up with only two or three possibilities, you probably need some more practice in creative problem-solving. If you came up with six or more, you're well on your way to turning an age-old conflict into a creative growth opportunity.

4.　Pressure from family, society, media to succeed.

Pressure to be successful comes from all directions — the media, family, friends, co-workers. Even the words we hear during childhood echo in our ears as we strive for success in the adult world.

The pressure can be as subtle as a friend or relative bragging on the success of a mutual acquaintance or as direct as a child's question, "Why don't we have a swimming pool like the Mitchells?"

Pressure to succeed is now finding its way into the preschool and kindergarten. Entrance exams and I.Q. tests for 2- and 3-year-old preschoolers are not uncommon in the higher-priced private schools, despite adequate evidence that such tests are unreliable during the early years.

A recent magazine article described what clothes and toys to buy your 5-year-old child to prepare him or her to take the kindergarten entrance tests. We are forcing children into a success/failure mode before they even have the opportunity to develop their talents and find out what they do well.

> *The danger we face as adults is in using someone else's yardstick to measure our own success. To do so is a prescription for frustration and failure.*

The problem with any measure of success — from first-grade report cards to annual profit-and-loss statements — is that no single measure fits everyone. The executive who is a good "idea person" may be a poor "detail person." The well-rounded college student may lack the impressive GPA of the devoted bookworm. A good team player may not be the one to score the winning touchdown.

You can no more measure creativity with a college board score than you can measure a person's weight with a yardstick. It just doesn't work.

A wise educator once reminded the parents of her gifted students that when they entered the business world, they would not be "ability grouped." They would be expected to know how to work with all kinds of people, to bring out the best in others, and to show leadership in groups of people with diverse talents, skills, and backgrounds. She knew that her students needed more than high achievement-test scores in order to be successful in life.

The danger we face as adults is in using someone else's yard-stick to measure our own success. To do so is a prescription for frustration and failure. Our friends may measure their success in ways that may or may not be relevant to our own lives: number of promotions, salary, golf handicap, frequent-flyer miles, etc.

Daniel's Story:

At one point in time, competition among our friends became so intense that success was measured in triglyceride and cholesterol levels. It was not enough simply to be financially successful and socially prominent. Even the status of your health was a competitive measure. It was not unusual to overhear people discussing the results of their recent physicals and lab tests in the never-ending race to be more physically fit than their friends.

In the popular movie, *City Slickers*, the crusty old cowboy tells the stressed-out young city slicker that the secret to life is "just one thing." Eager for a quick solution to his identity crisis, the city slicker demands to know, "What is it?"

The wise reply was: "That's what you have to figure out for yourself." Each of us has to figure out what our own measure of success will be, and then we can get about the business of achieving it.

5. Lack of proper training in the use of delegation, prioritizing and time management

Ask any successful business or professional person about the skills that are critical to effective performance. She or he will almost always include delegation, prioritizing and time management on the list.

Look at almost any educational curriculum leading to a business or professional degree, however, and you will find a peculiar absence of those same skills. If we assume that these critical skills are not a matter of genetic inheritance, then we may also assume that each of us enters the workplace lacking some of the tools that are critical to success.

Many businesses and professional organizations offer excellent continuing education and professional-development seminars on time management and other leadership skills. Such programs typically focus on how to apply these critical skills in the workplace, and do not expand the notion of management or leadership to a 24-hour day or whole-life model. The problem is that we are in fact whole people and that we usually do not become someone radically different during the hours we spend at work.

Leadership begins at home. A professional or executive who is not able to manage his or her 24-hour day will have more difficulty in managing the workday than someone who exhibits effective leadership in all aspects of life.

Unfortunately, there are even fewer training/learning opportunities for whole-life leadership than there are for the specific skills of prioritizing, delegation, and time management. A sixth (and closely related) external root cause of life imbalance is lack of training and experience in the Balanced Life Model for decision making.

6.   Lack of training in the Balanced Life Model for decision making.

Balanced life is a lot like parenting and marriage —very important jobs for which we have virtually no training! To complicate matters, the balanced-life skills we may have observed in parents or mentors may not be adequate for the situations we face today.

The holistic Balanced Life Model includes career development, health and leisure skills, personal relationship building and self-actualization and spiritual growth. If we learn these skills at all, they are likely to come in bits and pieces: a career-development seminar at work, a marriage or parenting workshop in the community, a weekend spiritual retreat at church. Nowhere do we have the opportunity to take our lives as complete wholes and develop the skills to address the big picture.

Dave:

Dave was an executive in retail management who found himself unable to handle even mild confrontations with his employees, despite having superior skills in other areas. The

problem was that his personal, career, leisure and self-fulfillment needs were all wrapped up in the job. His friends,
social activities, and self-esteem were all dependent on his
job and co-workers. He was reluctant to confront co-workers
who were also friends, and his job performance was suffering as a result.

Dave had received training in all the management skills, including conflict-resolution training. However, the skill he needed most as a manager was unknown to him. If he had been as skilled in managing his life as he was in balancing a budget, Dave would have known that having all of his personal needs tied to his work was risky not only for his personal well-being but for his job performance as well.

In Dave's situation, the solution to his problems with conflict resolution actually lay outside the workplace. When he was able to develop relationships and interests outside work, then conflicts at work were less threatening, and he was able to use his conflict-management skills more effectively.

The holistic approach of the Balanced Life Model may be compared to an effective long-range corporate development strategy. Each decision is evaluated in terms of its contribution to the overall mission of the organization as well as its immediate result or outcome.

The holistic approach of the Balanced Life Model may be compared to an effective long-range corporate development strategy. Each decision is evaluated in terms of its contribution to the overall mission of the organization as well as its immediate result or outcome. This approach to decision-making is leadership at its best.

In the Balanced Life Model, leadership begins at home, and good management begins with having an overall plan or mission for our own lives, one that includes our work, our relationships, our health and leisure, and our self-actualization and spiritual growth.

Internal Root Causes of Life Imbalance

Internal causes of life imbalance involve our own thinking, feeling and perceiving. How we react or respond to an external circumstance, such as a demand on our time, depends to a great deal on our internal belief system.

1. The achievement gap: "Always do your best."
2. The success gap: Of fact and fantasy
3. The internalized success model: Success = career achievement
4. The security gap: Internal security = financial security
5. Avoidance: Busy lifestyle provides shield from personal issues
6. False belief Number 1: I can/must "have it all"
7. False belief Number 2: I can/must "do it all"

1.   The achievement gap: "Always do your best."

A funny thing happens when we adhere to the old maxim, "Always do your best." When a worker puts forth a good effort and succeeds at a task, she or he is often rewarded by being presented with a more difficult task, higher expectations and a shorter time frame! Moving rapidly along this continuum of escalating expectations and diminishing resources, each worker eventually reaches his or her natural limit.

If the achievement gap is defined as the difference between achievement and capacity, most modern workers find themselves in a desperate race to close the gap. When the gap is finally closed (meaning that a person is working at near-maximum capacity), the worker's choice is to come to terms with her or his unique combination of gifts and limitations, or to continue to increase goals and expectations to the point of becoming ineffective and unproductive.

This process was described years ago as the "Peter Principle" — the process by which each worker is promoted to his or her highest level of incompetence.

Unless workers learn to be both realistic and selective about the tasks they undertake, closing the "achievement gap" will ultimately become a self-defeating process.

The co-author fondly recalls the first time she broke the

"Always do your best" rule. It was in graduate school that she was faced with the painful realization that she probably could not make her customary "A" average, hold down a part-time job and keep herself in clean laundry.

"I had reached a natural limit," Cecilia recalls. "The choice was painful but clear. I actively chose the classes in which I would invest maximum effort and expectation and those in which I would simply get by. The decision was both painful and productive.

"I utilize to this day some of the material and lessons from those classes to which I gave priority. If I had tried to 'do my best' in every single class, I would have been mediocre in everything."

2. The success gap: Of fact and fantasy

At some point (often around middle age), adults become acutely aware of time. Not only are there too few hours in the day, suddenly there is an awareness that there are not enough years in which to accomplish all the dreams of youth.

This awareness typically comes in two forms: negative comparisons with peers or relatives; and negative comparisons with one's own expectations, dreams, or fantasies.

The author's personal experiences have confirmed for him that negative comparisons with someone else's success create anxiety and a chronic sense of dissatisfaction, no matter how impressive or how long the list of one's personal achievements. For example, Madan explains:

> I look forward to visiting relatives in India. It is a pleasure to attend the weddings, and a joy to meet the nieces and nephews and see how they have grown since the last visit. Most of the relatives on both sides of the family have done well for themselves financially. One part of the visit I could do without are the conversations with the more affluent ones regarding how someone else has netted a "bigger deal" than they. As the conversation goes on, it becomes obvious that this comparison of achievements is stopping them from feeling good about their own accomplishments.

Because we live in a competitive world, it is normal for us to feel some anxiety in comparing our accomplishments to someone else's definition of success. The issue here is how we deal with it. Do we deal with it in a healthy or unhealthy way? Do we stay depressed? Do we continue to feel anxious? How long do we take to snap out of these negative feelings?

One way of dealing with the bad feelings engendered by these comparisons is to "pick up the pace." Becoming a workaholic allows us to mask the feelings of insecurity, but does not heal them. Developing broader and more appropriate personal goals for a balanced life — the big picture — is more likely to result in a genuine and lasting sense of satisfaction. Madan recalls:

> On the way back from a family vacation in Hawaii, we stopped in San Francisco to visit with a very close friend. Mark and I started careers at about the same time. Looking at his home and his position in the company, it was obvious that he was earning more than I was. On the flight home, the difference between his success and mine started to nag at me, resulting in feelings of anxiety and dissatisfaction.

Immediately on a napkin I drew the Balanced Life Model to answer the questions, "Am I getting out of my life what I want?" The results were both pleasing and surprising: Career — a career which challenges me, helps me grow, and in which I enjoy the respect of colleagues and superiors. People — a lovely wife, two healthy children, time to attend children's activities, and a good circle of friends. Actualization — lifestyle allows time to devote to reading and writing about balanced life, conduct workshops at nearby universities, participate in religious activities and nurture spiritual development. Leisure — twice-weekly tennis games with friends I love to be with, walks around the block with my wife several times a week. The C-PAL exercise enabled me to evaluate my own bottom line (not someone else's!) and to realize that what someone else is or has is of little relevance to my own life.

3.   The internalized success model: Success = career achievement

Like the "success gap," the internalized success model results from allowing others to take charge of our lives and set our priorities and expectations. We look around and find many "models" of success: prestige, money, houses, cars, vacations, corporate success, sales figures, social engagements, even our children's accomplishments.

The problem with accepting or internalizing someone else's measure of success is that it may not fit. Like a suit of clothes borrowed from a stranger, someone else's model of success just may not fit your unique combination of talents, abilities, and resources.

Using someone else's model of success, there will always be someone who has more or is "doing it better." Only by developing and using our own model of success, can we come up with life goals and activities that fit us so well that absolutely no one could "do it better."

> *Only by developing and using our own model of success, can we come up with life goals and activities that fit us so well that absolutely no one could 'do it better.'*

4. The security gap: Internal security = financial security

It is human need to want to feel secure externally as well as internally. We purchase elaborate security systems because we want to be secure against physical harm. We purchase life-insurance policies to secure ongoing support for our loved ones in case of untimely death.

We want to have peace of mind, a sense of security that our own and other family member's emotional, financial, and physical needs are being met and will continue to be met.

This search for absolute security in an uncertain world is not really a feasible proposition. Even when we achieve a respectable level of income, much more than what we start out with at the beginning of our careers, we don't feel so secure.

We think the reason for this feeling of insecurity is that we never make enough money. As the income grows, we assume larger mortgage payments to claim larger mortgage-interest deductions on the tax returns. Now, the bigger the mortgage, the greater the sense of insecurity.

We wanted our financial security so we could be free from worries, but the larger mortgage and car payments, in effect, restrict our freedom. To keep up with the bills, we have to work harder and longer. In this environment, the career self demands and consumes more and more hours resulting in an unbalanced lifestyle.

In a seminar, the author asked a group of business owners (people whose income levels put them in the top 1 percent of all wage earners in the country), "What are you after in life?" The answer from each was "financial security." If income levels such as theirs have not provided a sense of financial security, then the rest of us must surely be doomed!

Real internal security — as we've all experienced at least for brief moments — really comes from supporting and loving relationships with human beings, the Supreme being and the larger world beyond our office door.

> *Money is not required to buy one necessity of the soul.*
> — Henry David Thoreau

5.   Avoidance: Busy lifestyle provides shield from personal issues

It is easy to avoid thinking about our lives by staying in constant motion. If there is one word that seems to characterize the current generation, it is "busy." The constant motion appears to be a function of external causes — demands of career, family, finances, social obligations. However, it is actually an internal curse.

No one forces us to take on all these commitments. At some point, we chose each one. That's a shocking thought for many of us. It is a sobering exercise to think backward to the point in time at which we actually chose or accepted each of the commitments that now seem to be more burden than challenge: marriage, job, home, graduate school, church participation, civic leadership, children, travel, friendships, etc.

How did these once joyful choices become burdens? The problem lies not in the quality of the choices but in the method of choosing. No one taught us how to make choices, readjust priorities and adapt our lives to ever-changing economic and social realities. Instead, we choose *everything* and lose ourselves in the mad dash to keep up with it all.

The vicious cycle continues as we become so busy trying to fulfill all the commitments we have that there is no time to think about where our lives are going. Like a juggler we have so many objects in motion that we cannot move ourselves. We are rooted to the spot on which we stand by the knowledge that one false move or lapse of attention will bring things crashing down on our heads.

As those of us who can remember our last circus know, even the juggler has to stop and collect all the objects before he can do anything else. He does not try to start a new routine until he has finished the old one. He carefully collects all the balls, plates or pins, refocuses his attention and begins a new routine by introducing the objects into the air one at a time until he has reached all that he can manage.

Like the juggler, we must stop for a minute and collect ourselves if we are to be able to do anything except stand in one spot and juggle the same old things. Reflection is necessary for growth. The avoidance of reflection created by a too busy lifestyle is ultimately self-defeating.

Effort without purpose and direction becomes meaningless and unproductive. We may do much without any sense of accomplishment because we didn't know where we were headed in the first place!

It is important to take time to stop and reflect on our lives as wholes — work, relationships, leisure and fulfillment. There's nothing wrong with being busy so long as there is a sense of purpose to the effort.

6. False belief Number 1: I can/must "have it all"

We are all bombarded by the message, "You can have it all." After hearing it repeatedly, we internalize it and say to ourselves, "I *must* have it all." This message can be a positive motivator as long as the "all" is defined very, very carefully. The list that makes up "all" must be a very individual matter, and every item on the list may not be achieved simultaneously!

Operating under the belief system of "I must have it all," we wear ourselves out by running after the pieces that make up the picture of "all" in our minds. A media dream picture of "all" includes a successful career, regular promotions, a happy marriage, a grand home, multiple cars, impressive vacations, a circle of attractive friends, well-adjusted children who star in sports and make the honor roll, a Garden Club yard of the month, participation in social and civic organizations, a trim and tanned body, etc.

There is a sobering reality out there, however: the economy; a fiercely competitive work environment; only 24 hours in the day; the time period required for building a career often being the same time period in which children grow up; the aging human body, etc. It all gets in the way of "having it all," especially all at the same time.

Usually we look at people who are financially successful and assume she or he must "have it all." If we really knew all that is going on in that person's life, we might find a very different story.

The individual may be successful materially, but still may not feel secure or even financially successful. Personal health or family health may not be so good; relationships may not be prospering; or there may not be time to enjoy the hard-earned success. The appearance of "having it all" does not allow us to escape reality.

7.   False belief Number 2: I can/must "do it all"

The companion to "having it all" is "doing it all" — the pitfalls of which are apparent in this personal account from the co-author:

> One lovely morning in May, it happened: My child finished a nutritious breakfast without complaint, the baby-sitter arrived promptly, the beds were made, lunch and supper menus were prepared, my business suit was pressed and clean, my briefcase was filled with completed work, I had a stimulating conversation with my husband over breakfast and I left for work on time! Feeling contented and fulfilled, I pulled out of the driveway, marveling at how clever I had been to manage it all. Like King Arthur and his knights, I had created the perfect environment — my own Camelot!
>
> It would be at least six months, however, before I visited Camelot again. By the following week, the baby-sitter had

been called away to tend to a sick relative, my daughter had developed a fixation on nutrition-free cereals, my briefcase was bulging with unfinished work, my house was buried under a mountain of dust and laundry and four crisis-laden days in a row had left my husband with no time or energy for clever conversation. My own sense of cleverness vanished as quickly as it had come.

"Doing it all" was often held up as the ultimate achievement for women of the Eighties. What many of us found was that doing it all:

- Results in fatigue, which dulls the sense of accomplishment
- Cannot be sustained over a long period

When we are too tired and frustrated from trying to "do it all," we feel chronically behind and frustrated no matter how much we achieve. Our many worthy successes are summarily sacrificed on the funeral pyre of our failures.

The Camelot story affects men in a different way. Reared on personal and media role models of corporate success and little in the way of home responsibilities, they are now coming home to wives who have been at work all day. Both partners tend to arrive home late, tired and preoccupied, wishing desperately that the "dinner fairy" would appear and put a hot meal on the table. Men too are often pressured to "do it all" without slowing their climb up the corporate ladder. Stress-related illnesses, career burnout, chemical abuse and family conflict are among the prices paid for trying to do it all.

What about Camelot? Is it necessary to give up dreams in order to develop workable roles and goals? Is it possible for one person to actually enjoy his or her career, family and personal life? It is not necessary to give up dreams, but a few dream-management strategies are necessary to bridge the gap between fiction and reality.

Here is the sequel to the co-author's Camelot story:

I have become better at sequencing and prioritizing roles. I can do it all — but not all at the same time! I ask for help and receive it. I accept my children's version of a cooked meal or a clean room in exchange for not having to do it myself. I have become willing to pay more attention to my successes than to my failures. Life here in the real world can be fun and fulfilling without being perfect.

I have also learned to enjoy those "brief shining moments" when it all comes together. I know those moments will not last forever, but I also know they will surely come again.

40 Practical Ideas for Developing Your Personal Balanced Life Plan

To live in the present does not imply rashness or irresponsibility or selfishness; it is not an act of hedonism or of cowardly escape. It is to live with instant appreciation of the good in life and in freedom from obsessive anxiety.

— Charles Morgan

WE DRIFT INTO A WAY OF LIFE and may never find out until it is too late that it wasn't the kind of life we wanted. This happens when we follow the "psychology of more:"

- "I'll spend more time with the family after I receive this promotion."
- "We'll be happy when we build that house."
- "If I can get just one more contract, I will have it made and I can quit worrying about the Visa payment."

When we live for tomorrow, the present eludes us.

This chapter will present specific ideas and tools to help you develop a personal balanced-life action plan that allows time for career, relationships, leisure and actualizing activities in a balanced manner on a weekly basis, if not on a daily basis.

Invariably, the root causes of life imbalance reflect a combination of the internal as well as the external. The solution will involve dealing with both — changes in values within to address the internal root causes, as well as relationships with the outer world to address the external root causes.

Intellectual understanding without action will not result in changes needed to regain the balanced life. Action without understanding results in shallow or short-lived change. Both have to be addressed. One won't work without the other.

CAUTION: *Do not* try to use all of these ideas at once! Go back to Chapter 3 on Root Causes of Life Imbalance and identify the most important causes of imbalance in your own life. Then select the practical ideas that will help you most effectively address the sources of imbalance.

Each idea has a "think" and a "do" component to help you address both internal and external issues as you develop your own plan. Finally, enjoy your own creativity and add your own ideas to the list.

1. Reclaiming Your Life One Day at a Time — Making Your Calendar Work for You

Think ... of your calendar as representing your life, not just your list of work obligations, appointments and commitments to others.

Do ... Schedule the People, Actualizing and Leisure activities *first* on the monthly calendar before scheduling business appointments and career activities.

> I remember being one of the few fathers at the school talent shows. The joy shared at these moments cannot be described in words. I look at the conflict between work and family in these situations as follows: If I can find the time to be with my child when she or he is sick, surely I can find time to share his or her joyous moments. Most of us in the professional ranks are paid for the quality of our decisions/work and not by the hour. We can include family and personal time in our work day.
>
> — Madan Birla

> When I was taping my show at NBC Burbank, I left between shows to attend my son's Little League games some 10 miles away. It meant so much to him to see his father in the stands. I do the same today for my grandson. I never missed my daughter's plays or recitals. As busy as we are, there is still time to invest in your family. As a result, we are as close today as our family could be.
>
> — Monty Hall
> TV Game Show Host

2. Share Your Balanced Life Priorities and Action Plans with People in Your Life

Think ... of how it is a wrong assumption to believe that you know what your significant other's and childrens' priorities are. Ask them, "Are my priorities in synchronization with yours?" Even if you knew what these were a year ago, they change as people grow. Balanced-life plans must be regularly updated and discussed with those close to you.

Do ... allow others to remind you of your balanced-life plan! Once you have told your children that the family will be going somewhere for the weekend, they won't let you forget that. With all the demands on our time, it is good to have someone reminding us of our own balanced-life plans.

3. Say 'No' to Requests and Activities in Conflict with Your Balanced-Life Plans

I am criminally well-organized and I prioritize (what a dreadful word!). Friends, husband, job, sex, family ... all the important things I fit in. Peripheral stuff that has to be taken care of — the house, Christmas presents for people who help you all year long, dental, doctor, hairdressing — I also fit in. Since I like work so much better than play — for me work is play — I don't have to worry about tennis, sun-bathing, racquetball, rock-climbing, etc. There are plenty of other things I don't fit in that people pester you to do. I am able to say "no" ruthlessly. We're back to my first thoughts — organization and prioritization (gracious, how dull!) are the only things that allow balance in life."

> — Helen Gurley Brown
> *Cosmopolitan* Magazine

Think ... about the message here. Unless we watch what we obligate ourselves to do, we can easily lose our life balance. Don't try to be everything socially that's not you.

Do ... evaluate *each* request on your time and energy in terms of your personal goals and balanced-life plans.

> *Unless we watch what we obligate ourselves to do, we can easily lose our life balance. Don't try to be everything socially that's not you.*

4. Be Continually Aware of the Blessings in Life

Think ... about how the success gap is such a powerful negative force waiting to disturb the life balance, especially in successful and achievement-oriented people.

We tend to take the most valuable things in life — health, love of family, supportive friends, evening walks, successful projects/accomplishments at work — for granted. Taking stock and being aware provides a solid foundation and the right attitude to successfully deal with the problems.

To remember that who we are and what we become has its roots in our childhood. To know that what is essential is invisible to the eye. To believe that the Creator of the Universe cares about each one of us in a unique and loving way.

— Fred Rogers
Mr. Rogers Neighborhood

Do ... start each day by taking a moment to reflect on something or someone for which you are thankful. If you tend to forget the positives, *write them down* in your calendar, diary or journal.

5. Do Things for People Less Fortunate Than You

Think ... about the world beyond your home and office walls ... about your place in the universe rather than your position in the office ... about what you have to share with others and what others have shared with you.

Do ... things for people who are less fortunate than you are. There are so many such people, and you will be amazed at the positive effects you experience.

Visit a hospital, homeless shelter, and it makes me realize

that I am fortunate to have my problems, because with God's help I can solve them. This works for me whether I'm on a roll or depressed.

> — Lou Holtz
> Former Head Coach,
> University of Notre Dame

This helps us in the action plan discussed in Number 4 above. We all write checks for United Way, American Cancer Society and other charitable organizations. But there is a special joy in doing things firsthand and reaching out to others in person.

6.   Minimize Financial Worries by Living Within Your Means

Think ... about how credit cards, equity loans and store financing make it easy to buy this and replace that. Living from paycheck to paycheck creates a tremendous sense of financial insecurity and creates tension in relationships. Both conditions impact balanced life in a very negative way.

> I experienced this feeling when I was laid off from my first job after only three months. Fortunately, I was able to get another job within a month. But since then, I've saved and put away funds for covering all home expenses for at least a year. I remember a friend who within a month of losing his job, saw his wife leave him, too. The pile of bills and no income was just too much stress for the relationship to handle.
>
> — Madan Birla

Do ... learn how to make choices. Discuss those choices and teach your children how to make them as well. (As in: We can eat out twice a week or we can take turns cooking at home and save the money for that trip we've all been wanting).

7.   Use the Balanced-Life Model's C-PAL Circle to Remind and Reinforce the Balanced Lifestyle and to Counteract 'Make It' Pressures

Think ... about your whole life and not just your job.

The focus point of my life is my daughter and wife. I derive my strength and enthusiasm for my work from their love and encouragement. When I place my family first and everything else behind them, then I am able to maintain my life balance.

— President Bill Clinton

Do ... draw the C-PAL circle on a piece of paper every six months or so and review each of the components to make sure your current lifestyle is celebrating life in its fullness.

8.   Notecard Exercise: An Excellent Tool for Enhancing Relationships On and Off the Job

Think ... about how we tend to assume that family, friends and co-workers automatically know what you appreciate about them. In our busy lifestyle, we do not take time to tell each other the good things.

Do ... get the family or work group together and pass out a clean sheet of paper to each member. Ask each person to complete the following sentence: "I like you or I appreciate you because ..." for everyone in the group including himself or herself. After everyone is finished writing, each person reads aloud her or his compliments. If there are six persons in a group, then each member gets to hear six beautiful compliments.

Collect all the sheets and have each person's compliments typed on a blank note card. You can carry a card in your briefcase and read them whenever you need a lift.

9.   Share Experiences and Not Just Things

Think ... about the last time you shared an important experience with someone close to you. Remember that gifts are no substitute for shared experiences.

You wanted to know how I maintain a balance between my professional and personal life. I must tell you that time with my family is vital to me. Although it is sometimes difficult, I make it a point to spend as much time as possible with my wife and two daughters. In fact, I make it a point to be with my family on our birthdays and holidays, regardless of my professional schedule.

— Tom Harkins
United States Senator

A few years back on a flight from Memphis to Las Vegas, the author was sitting next to a high school teacher from Las Vegas. Conversation revealed that the teacher and his family were returning to Las Vegas after visiting the New Orleans World Fair. During a discussion on balanced-life issues, he shared his philosophy.

He said, "I have a daughter in high school, and we try to do as many things as we can as a family. To afford trips like this on a teacher's salary, it means continuing to drive and repair my old car. I believe it is more important to share experiences than things."

Do ... look on your calendar and see if you have each member of your family listed by name at least once this month. Even something as simple as "read a book to Suzie," or "watch Mark's new break-dance routine" will help you make time to share experiences.

10. So What if it Takes 10 Years to Learn and/or Get Into Something You Would Really Like to Do?

Think ... about walking a mile one step at a time. How many times during the course of a year do you hear someone or even yourself say, "Oh, how I wish I could do that," or "What I'd really like to do is ..."?

One solution to this kind of thinking came in a career counseling class: "If you get started today, you'll be there two years from now. Otherwise you'll still be saying the same thing next year and the year after that." In our instant-gratification culture, it is very difficult to have that much patience. However, because the average life span is now more than 70 years, we do have the opportunity for more than one career.

As a matter of fact, the seeds for this book were sown 10 years ago when one of the authors enrolled in a counseling degree program while working as a manager! Although we don't exactly know the path that life will take over a 10-year period, if we get started, there is a good chance that we'll get there. Goals leading to self-actualization are worth the effort, because in the process we discover and celebrate who we really are.

Do ... identify a small step toward one of your life goals and start working on it *today.*

11. Allow Time for Developing and Expressing Your Spiritual Dimension

Think ... about your values. Your spirituality may involve prayer, meditation, nature or other activities. Do not assume that spirituality is reserved only for those who belong to churches or organized religious groups. Spirituality is a part of each human being. In order for life to be whole, all the pieces must be there. Otherwise, there is a vacuum.

> I suspect if proper balance in life is to be maintained, there should be a standard of high moral values at all times, respect for family, church affiliation, work enjoyment, and community involvement.
>
> — Sam Walton
> Founder of Wal-Mart

Do ... find others with whom you can share and discuss your values. Put your values into practice. Notice the values that are reflected in your calendar and your checkbook.

If you get started today, you'll be there two years from now. Otherwise you'll still be saying the same thing next year and the year after that.

12. Enjoy the Moment: Do Fun Things Today

Think ... about the following comments made by a participant after attending the Leadership and Balanced Life seminar: "A tiny delicate flower may seem insignificant by itself but can color a hillside in sufficient numbers. Small pleasures and rewards can add up to fulfillment if repeated."

Do ... make plans and share them with others.

In my family, it is a must that we have a family activity every week in which the whole family participates:

movie, play, Putt-Putt, bowling, picnic, outing, etc. Although my teenage son would often try to get out of it, it was him who reminded me this summer (before he went away to college) that it was time to renew our family subscription to Theater Memphis.

— Madan Birla

13. Keep Your Life Values and Priorities in Focus All the Time

Before founding Mary Kay Cosmetics, I had over 25 years experience in the direct selling field. In working with women, I found that the most important things in their lives were their faiths and their families, with their careers taking third place. After retiring in 1963, I decided to start my own company, hoping to give women a work opportunity that would offer them a chance to keep their priorities in the proper order. Our company philosophy became and remains today — "God first, family second, career third." Our Beauty Consultants work the hours they choose. Today our sales force is nearing a quarter of a million, and it has been said we have more women earning over $50,000 and even $100,000 a year than any other company in America. Our top people can earn this kind of money and still keep their lives in balance!

— Mary Kay Ash
Founder, Mary Kay Cosmetics

14. Develop and Use Your Faith

Think ... of how spiritual faith provides the foundation for optimism. Psychological studies have shown that optimistic people with talent do better than pessimistic people with similar talent.

All that I have seen teaches me to trust the Creator for all that I have not seen.

— Ralph Waldo Emerson
19th Century American Essayist

Do ... discriminate between what you can and cannot control. If it is helpful, make a list of your worries, then separate it into what you can and cannot control. Use your spiritual and faith development to let go of what you cannot control.

15. Talk Out Your Worries

Think ... how lack of time and energy — the two personal resources — stops us from leading balanced lifestyles. Worrying saps more energy than physical exertion.

Do ... acknowledge personal problems. This is difficult for individuals who have always relied on their independence. Talking to a trusted friend or a relative can help you sort things out. Men especially need to guard against thinking, "I'm not supposed to have self doubts."

16. Avoid Irritating and Overly Competitive People

Think ... of how we tell our kids to be careful about the type of company they keep because we are concerned about their being influenced negatively — drugs, alcohol, anti-social behavior, etc. Yet even we as grownups are influenced by the kind of company we keep. Overly competitive people always want to win at work and often even at play. Competing in everything and with everybody is not conducive to building relationships.

Do ... pay attention to your personal "barometers" that tell you if the company you are keeping is enhancing your life or detracting from it. When the social party debates become heated and personal, the party that was supposed to be a light and fun evening leaves you mad and drained. Limit your contact with people and situations that leave you feeling drained, tense or irritated.

17. Take Time to Talk to Yourself for Learning from the Greatest Teacher: Life

Think ... of how psychologists once said that if you talked to yourself you were not OK mentally. Now we know that to stay in touch with ourselves, we need to have some inner dialogue

Do ... ask, "Am I getting out of life what I want?" Also, we need to listen to the unmet needs of the different dimensions of the self. This requires us to be still periodically, as the outside and the inner "noise" can drown out this small voice.

18. Take Time to Pamper Yourself

Think ... about how you feel when you do take time (even for just a few minutes) for yourself. Consider the following conversation with the spouse of a successful executive:

> After I send the kids to school, I go to my husband's office. In the evening, I cook, clean and put the kids to bed. Weekends are busy with soccer games, shopping ... I just don't have time to do anything myself.
> Q. How does that make you feel?
> A. Resentful at times.
> Q. Are you a better person to be around when you are not resentful?
> A. Of course I am!

Psychological studies have shown that optimistic people with talent do better than pessimistic people with similar talent.

Do ... put time for yourself on your calendar and give it priority!

19. Delegate, Delegate, Trust, Trust

Think ... about the fact that one of the key skills of a successful manager is delegation. In reality, most managers under-delegate and thus overload themselves. Since there are only 24 hours in a day, the extra hours taken for work have to come out of the other three components: People, Actualization and Leisure.

Do ... delegate tasks at work. It is not only good life balance, it is good management.

> The experience of learning over the years to delegate and then seeing the results and then delegating more and seeing the results and really building a good team around you, where you are in a position where you're not trying to do their job for them because they don't want you trying to do their job for them. They shouldn't be there if you don't have total confidence in their ability to do the job.
> Somebody asked me a question a couple weeks ago at a

social function. We had been talking a bit about what we did for a living — you know, who we work for and what our jobs were and all that other stuff, and they said, "How in the world do you stay on top? You've got 90,000 people ... blah blah blah ... How do you sleep at night?"

I said, "I sleep like a baby." They looked at me like "Huh?" and I repeated, "I sleep like a baby." Then I explained, "The Senior Vice Presidents that we have at our company — I'm speaking especially about my group, but they are all the same way — are absolute top-notch. They're doing a terrific job, and on a day-to-day basis I never worry about what are they doing out there to screw up. It doesn't enter my mind because I know that they are very proactive, are making the right kind of decisions and the right things happen. I do — I sleep like a baby.

If through reports and conversation I see a trend that may concern me or something like that, then I'll pick up the phone and say, "What's going on? There is something here that I want to know about and etc., etc." Frankly, those are pretty few and far in between.

— Bill Razzouk
Executive Vice President,
Federal Express Corporation

Do ... delegate tasks at home. It is not only good life balance, it is good parenting!

A busy physician and father of four commented about his children's rooms: "Of course, they are not as neat as I would keep them. The point is that they are learning responsibility, and I am not spending my valuable family time putting away toys!"

20. The Weekly Schedule Must Include Some Time for Just the Two of You

From the start of my marriage, my wife, Arvella, and myself have made the commitment to have a weekly date night with each other. Every Monday night is reserved on my calendar for her. When the children were young, we left them with a baby-sitter. Now that all five of our children are grown and married, they have adapted "date night" into their lives as well.

— Robert Schuller

21. Sequence

Think ... about what you want to accomplish over your lifetime, rather than what you want to cram into the next few weeks. Consider that you may not be able to achieve all your goals simultaneously, but may be able to attain most of them during your lifetime.

We cannot give top priority to everything at once. Yet most of us do not relish the idea of having to choose between family and career. One way out of this dilemma is to sequence priorities:

- Delaying starting a family to devote time to career;
- Slowing down the career track when children are young;
- Putting in overtime in order to have a three-day weekend;
- Adding more household help during peak workloads;
- Reducing expenditures in order to reduce overtime and increase family time;
- Buying a new house and driving an old car;
- Driving a new car and keeping the old house;
- Skipping the vacation this year to save for the big trip next year.

Sequencing priorities is critically important in the lives of women, who are vulnerable to feeling chronically torn between home and career.

In my early 20s, my fantasy was to have a house, a Ph.D., a Mercedes-Benz and a baby. The car came first — a used foreign car was manageable on two incomes and no children! The Ph.D. came next, but was interrupted by the arrival of our first child. By the time the Ph.D. was finished, the foreign car was gone, replaced by an unpaid student loan and a family station wagon. Later came home ownership and another child. Looking back, it all worked out well

— just not all at the same time!

— Cecilia Marshall

Do ... keep your priorities before you. Write them down if necessary. Evaluate them regularly and change them when needed.

22. Take Occasional Unplanned Long Weekends

Think ... always that creativity is the key to keeping relationships (the People component) alive.

Do ... be creative in finding destinations within the town where you live or within a four hour drive.

You may not be able to achieve all your goals simultaneously, but may be able to attain most of them during your lifetime.

23. Use the C-PAL Circle to Evaluate and Focus on the Changing Needs of People in Your Life

Think ... about how all things in nature want to grow. If a tree is not growing, it is dead.

Each member of the family has the same four needs as you do, but the content and proportion of those needs change over time. The People Self in a 5-year-old needs the constant assurance of parents that she or he is somebody to somebody. When the child becomes a teenager, the peers occupy a larger role in the desire to be somebody to somebody. It is not that teenagers truly want to make parents' lives miserable. But painful conflicts often arise as they attempt to meet their changing "I want to be somebody" needs.

Do ... listen to the balanced-life needs of others in your family. Do discuss how you can encourage and enjoy each other's growth rather than being threatened by it.

24. Give Yourself Positive Strokes/Rewards for Leading a Balanced Life — Because the Outside World Does Not

Think ... of how a balanced life provides its own rewards and its own reinforcement. The pulls in the media and environment are toward leading an unbalanced life. By giving ourselves positive strokes, we strengthen the inner core and are less negatively influenced by the external forces.

Do ... Reward yourself with mental recognition, books, movies, a chess game, a concert, spiritual retreat. Spend time with other people who share your values and exchange positive strokes. Read books that support and reinforce your values and spiritual commitments.

25. Re-Evaluate Your Goals

Think ... that if you are tormented by unrealized career and material goals, you need to evaluate the goals to see if they are realistic and achievable.

The reality of the corporate world is that there is less and less room at the higher levels of the organizational pyramid. You may have the necessary skills and desire to be the vice president or president of the company; but it may not be achievable if the incumbent is not going to move.

The C-PAL Circle reminds us to look at the career as one part of this multi-dimensional life, versus letting life be completely dominated by career. It is good to have goals, as long as they are a source of positive motivation. However, if the reality of economics or competition is making them unreachable, we need to step back and reassess the situation.

In a recent seminar on connections between work and family, there were several family counselors present. They commented that they are seeing more and more people suffering with the ill effects of the "making it" pressures. These are people who are successful in other people's eyes, but have not yet achieved the higher goals they set for themselves.

Do ... use the C-PAL Circle as a tool to help you maintain (or regain) your sense of proportion.

26. Have a Place for Retreat at Home — Workshop, Garden, Study, Etc.

Think ... of the human need to get away from the pressures of "being somebody." The word "recreation" literally means "to be created again." This is how we feel when we are refreshed by a hobby or creative outlet, a new idea gained from reading or a change of pace.

Refinishing furniture: getting dirty and messy is a great relief — the product of one's own hands is always better.

Lynn Martin
Former U.S. Secretary of Labor

Do ... something!

27. Use All Your Vacation Days

One hears often in the corporate world: "I have not taken a vacation in so many years." She or he may think that he is doing the company a favor by not taking the allowed vacations. In reality, the company may be losing out on the employee's creative input. Vacations play a very important role. Time off from work recharges the battery and helps clean the cobwebs so creative ideas do become accessible.

Also, vacations with family and friends help by sharing experiences. Not all vacation days have to be used for long or out-of-town trips.

I get four weeks vacation. Two weeks are planned as family trips out of town. The other two, I just take one or two days at a time. Some days I schedule when schools are closed for one day holidays. Since my wife has just started a new job, she does not get four weeks. So on such days, I just plan a day in town with my daughter and her friends. On our last such outing, we went to Pizza Hut for lunch and then to the bowling alley. These are the girls I have known since they were 2 years old. It is just a sheer joy to see how delightful and interesting these young ladies have become. To share this joy, one just has to be around to listen and observe.

Also, on some vacation days, I just spend the whole day at the library to catch up on magazine articles.

— Madan Birla

Think ... of the fact that you have earned those vacation days. They are yours. So use them — if only for one-day outings.

Do ... use these days off to share yourself with the loved ones. Use these days to do the things you love to do but can't find the time — even if it means doing nothing!

28. Stop and Look at the Family Photos in the Office

Most of us have pictures of our families in the office. In the drive to empty the In-basket, there is not much free time left. In the drive to accomplish, it is easy to forget who we are working so hard for. When you are busy, the time just flies.

The trouble comes when years just fly, and before you know it the little boy is taller than you are. We need something and somebody to remind us that there are things for which we must take time out now because they won't be available later.

The family pictures in the office are waiting to remind us that this little boy or girl is growing up fast. We need to share and assist in important events before they are all grown up.

Do ... stop and look at the family pictures and notice how fast the kids are growing. If you keep reflecting on that regularly, then it won't be hard to leave the office for two hours in the middle of the day to be at the school play or the piano recital.

29. Loosen Up on the Cleanliness Standard

For most families, middle-class status is achieved by having two incomes. The demands of the day job, raising children and maintaining the household does not leave much time or energy for anything else. In this environment it is essential that you loosen up on the cleanliness standard for the house. Trying to maintain an absolutely clean house drains energy and uses up precious time.

Do ... loosen up on the cleanliness standard and use that small amount of free time for taking a walk (L), going to a movie with a friend (P), reading the book you've been wanting to read (L), or playing with the kids (P, L).

30. Use the Drive Time to and from Work to Concentrate on What is Important

The key to minimizing the briefcase of office work with you in the evening is to complete the important work while at the office. So on the drive to work, in addition to making a mental list of the "to-do" items, also reflect on what you're not going to waste your time on — the unimportant things.

Use the drive from office to home in the evening to concentrate on what is important when you get home. Remembering what you did right, versus focusing on what you could have done better or did not get to, helps put a smile on your face as you walk through the door. What is important in the evening is to acknowledge everyone in the home with a smile as you walk through the garage door.

> *Remembering what you did right, versus focusing on what you could have done better or did not get to, helps put a smile on your face as you walk through the door.*

It is through everyday behavior that we tell people what is really important to us. Of course, it is the people in our life! But if the work worries are creating an environment for the people in your life to wonder what mood you'll be in today, it is time to take some action.

31. Clear Communication with the Significant Other

Angie and Craig both have successful careers and two preschool children. Angie was feeling resentful because she felt that Craig was not doing his part in helping with the children and the homework. The problem, as she described it, she had been expecting Craig to read her mind. Now she writes down her expectations and communicates clearly the tasks on which she needs Craig's help.

32. Use the Lunch Hour for Running Errands

Make a list of your errands and use the lunch hour to run as many errands as you can. This will free up time after work in the evening and on weekends to spend with family or for doing things you like to do.

33. Use Technology

After the birth of her first child, Sandy, a management consultant, bought a home computer with a modem connected to her company's computer. This allowed her to work from home, and she demonstrated to her supervisors that she was equally productive there. She scheduled two half days at the office each week for face-to-face interaction. The flexibility she gained was worth the investment.

In the information economy, most professionals can do a good part of their job from home with the use of personal computers and fax machines. Most corporations do not want to lose the expertise and experience their people have, and are open to these arrangements.

34. Reduce Trips to the Supermarket
To make sure all the needed items are bought during the weekly trip to the supermarket, Cathy has computerized the grocery list. A copy is posted on the refrigerator. Everyone in the family circles the items as they are used up and need to be replenished.

35. We Cannot Do All Things — So Hire Help
One of the things I admire in America is the interest and the ability of people to fix things around the house. But as we assume more responsibility at work, and family obligations increase, there simply is not enough time to do every thing. This "to-do" overload can cut into People and Leisure time. One solution is to hire help for some of the routine chores.

36. Less Time in the Kitchen
Sam and Denise do their weekly cooking on Sunday afternoons for the whole week. Some dishes are cooked completely, while others are cooked partially. This way, whoever gets home first can get started toward having the dinner ready. Some days they pick up a dish from the deli or the health-food store.

37. Keeping Romance Alive
Next Friday, ask your significant other to meet you for lunch. Give sufficient notice so that he or she can make arrangements to get away for the afternoon. Before leaving your office for lunch write down on a blank card the five things you like about him or her.

After lunch, catch an afternoon movie. After the movie, share a cup of coffee and conversation or a stroll by the lake or through the park.

You may be saying to yourself that you cannot leave the office and "waste time" like this. Trust me, the business will not shut down because you are only going to put in 56 hours this week instead of the regular 60 hours. Suppose you were coming down with the flu — you could leave the office for the afternoon then, couldn't you?

The best use of time in life is the time we waste on people we love.

38. Say Aloud: It is Important to Me

You may have noticed by now that many of the practical ideas discussed here are fairly simple. The challenge is to put them into practice in your life. As discussed many times so far in the book the key to a successful balanced-life effort is the internal resolve to say to yourself: "It is important to me, and I am going to take time to do this."

39. Read and Reflect on Spiritual Material Every Day

Even if it is only for five minutes a day, the benefit in terms of internal strength and peace will be far greater than from anything else you could do in five minutes. You will have access to more of your inner resources and learn from the wisdom of the spiritually enlightened souls through their writings.

40. Ask Regularly: "Am I Getting Out of Life What I Want?"

How much fulfillment or enjoyment we get out of life is the direct result of how we are living our life. So if we are not getting out of life what we want, then we need to examine how we are living our life and identify the changes we need to make.

● ● ●

There is no "perfect" balance, and no one is able to sustain the balance over the long periods. But the effort itself will make the journey more enjoyable.

Do not try to change everything overnight. Just pick out one idea or activity and implement it for at least two weeks. Then pick out and implement another idea. Take your time.

5

11 Principles and Practices to Unleash Your Leadership and Creativity

Supported by authority, rules and regulations, you can get people to work at 60 to 65 percent capacity — just enough to satisfy minimum job requirements. Leadership is a multiplier factor that deals with the other 35 to 40 percent. A mere administrator can achieve average results. The leader gets superior results from average people. Management is largely an action-oriented cerebral process. Leadership is principally an action-oriented inter-personal process.
— **James J. Cribbin**, AMA, New York
Leadership: Strategies for Organizational Efficiency

CORPORATE SUCCESS AND PROFITABILITY in this highly competitive global economy will depend primarily on three conditions: ongoing practical innovation, quality products, and a true customer service orientation. Customer satisfaction, which is the critical factor in a corporation's success, will be achieved only through continuous improvements in each of these areas. These improvements will only come through the discretionary efforts of committed employees.

The most basic task of corporate leaders is to unleash the human spirit that makes initiative, creativity and entrepreneurship possible. In their article, "Changing the Role of Top Management: Beyond Systems to People," published in the May-June 1995 issue of the *Harvard Business Review*, Christopher Bartlett and Sumantra Ghosal discussed this.

Johnson & Johnson, General Electric, Intel, Allied Signal and Federal Express, among others, are some of the well-recognized companies known for quality products, services and superior customer service. Being a part of the Federal Express management team for more than 15 years has given me the opportunity to understand the key role of discretionary effort. Founder Fred

Smith's idea combined with employees who gave it all have created a new industry.

The findings of the customer surveys conducted by the Federal Express Marketing Department show that enthusiastic employees are key to superior customer service. When asked, "What is the number-one thing you like about doing business with Federal Express?" the response consistently has been: "the people we deal with" — not the planes or the sophisticated information systems or the complex package-sorting systems.

All other express-delivery companies have people too. What is so unique about Federal Express employees? The difference, according to the survey responses, is their enthusiasm — the key to providing superior customer service. This is demonstrated in their commitment to the success of the corporation, and thus to the quality of its products and services.

All employees are people first. No matter where they work, they have the same basic human attributes and potential for enthusiasm, innovation, and commitment. The reason these qualities are so visible in Federal Express employees is because tapping employee enthusiasm and commitment was both a corporate and a personal goal of Fred Smith and his management team from the very beginning of the company. It was a conscious strategy backed by solid action.

The majority of people in the management ranks throughout the corporate world have completed many years of formal education and also have years of experience in their field. They have attended many seminars and have read any number of books regarding state-of-the-art business practices. However, despite being so highly trained, they face real difficulties in applying their expertise and realizing their leadership and creative potential.

In computer terminology, management training and education can be thought of as the software. The information about a business problem is the input data. The manager is the central processing unit who must make productive use of the information.

To reap the full benefit of the training, the manager has to understand the micro-circuitry that forms his inner self. In other words, he has to understand who he is — his values, priorities, strengths and weaknesses. He must understand the sources of his motivation — his belief system, which works like a computer's operating system, directing the allocation of the manager's time and energy.

The successful manager *must* be deeply in tune with her or his inner self.

> Today's brutal competition favors the swift executives thoroughly in touch with themselves who can respond faster. The most important trait of a good leader is knowing who you are.
>
> — Edward McCracken, CEO
> Silicon Graphics

One of the greatest impediments to any manager's full use of his inner resources and managerial training is the lack of understanding and integration of the various pieces of this multi-dimensional inner self. To be truly successful over the long term, a manager must continue to be an integrated whole person.

The following 11 principles and practices will help you expand the understanding of your self. When applied, this self knowledge will enhance your personal effectiveness by unleashing the leadership skills and creativity you already possess.

1.   Shared Vision and Discretionary Effort

Leaders develop a vision of where the organization needs to go. They tap the discretionary effort — enthusiasm, commitment and creativity — from their inner self and from others in the organization to turn the vision into a reality. People willingly give extra effort when their leader makes them *feel* appreciated as valued members of a team going after the shared vision. Leadership, for both the leader and the follower, is more an affair of the heart than of the head.

2.   Love and the Human Heart

Love is to the human heart what the sun is to flowers. Development of love and deeper relationships requires time. So when we take time with the significant people in our lives to work on problems together, we have fun in the process. By communicating, and just being open to share the joys and sorrows, we are also unleashing our leadership potential.

3. Interpersonal and Intrapersonal

Our interpersonal skills (how we deal with others) are directly related to our intrapersonal skills (how we deal with ourselves). It is very difficult to be sensitive to the feelings of others if we are not sensitive to our own. We think we can, and we keep trying to separate the person from the manager. However, we are not successful, because how we are as a person very much affects our performance as a manager. A leader's first responsibility is to get in touch with himself.

> *Leadership, for both the leader and the follower, is more an affair of the heart than of the head.*

4. Know and Feel

Human behavior, what one knows and how one feels are all interrelated. Any two of these three factors influence the third. A manager may understand intellectually the need to make changes but if he feels insecure, the manager is not going to try and implement new ideas because of the risks involved. Being in touch with your inner sense of who you are provides the necessary confidence for risk taking.

5. Inner Security

Inner security comes from many sources. Some of the most important sources are a continuously updated knowledge base, proven abilities, supportive relationships and spiritual growth. All of these source areas can only be developed and sustained by devoting time to them on a regular basis.

6. Being at Peace

We are most creative and open to new ideas from within and from others when we are at peace. Being at peace means being in touch with and meeting the needs of all four dimensions of the Total Self — Career Self, People Self, Actualizing Self (spiritual) and Leisure Self.

7. Creativity in Action

A creative decision making process involves first visualizing the various alternatives, analyzing them and then selecting a preferred course of action from these alternatives. Psychological, emotional and non-rational factors influence this process. An agitated mind produces a distorted picture.

8. Energy and an Unbalanced Life

An unbalanced life creates internal conflict and negative feelings that use up the inner energy and enthusiasm necessary for being an effective leader. Some of the more common energy-absorbing conditions include feeling pessimistic, insecure or in conflict. Conversely, some of the more common energy-boosting conditions include feeling optimistic, secure or in harmony.

9. In Harmony

Management is a team sport. A manager who is not in harmony with himself cannot fully cooperate with others. Unresolved personal issues and an unchecked ego act as a dam on the flow of creative intelligence from the inner self and from others on the team.

10. Reflection and Learning

Reflection is key to lifelong learning and self understanding. Energy, creativity, and happiness flourish when through reflection a person's outer life is a willing and knowing expression of his inner life, personal values and priorities.

11. Two Kinds of Education

All of us need two kinds of education: one on how to make a living and the other on how to live a balanced life based on solid values and priorities. We are not born with the secret of how to live.

Taking a Closer Look

Let us take a more detailed look at each of the eleven principles and practices discussed.

1. Shared Vision and Discretionary Effort

Most managers typically favor left-brain activities. However, leadership skills call upon the right hemisphere of the brain. The left hemisphere works with facts, and a logical, point-by-point thinking. The right hemisphere works with feelings, intuition, and image building.

Psychological research tells us that the left side of the brain is the place for segmented, analytical and rational processes. The right side supports conceptual, creative and feeling processes. Our analytical side makes us good planners, organizers and controllers — and thus, effective *managers*. Our feeling and conceptual side makes us visionary, caring and inspiring managers — and thus, effective *leaders*.

An overly intellectual, heartless person never becomes an inspired person or an inspiring manager. Just as the intellect is the instrument of knowledge, so is the heart the instrument of inspiration.

Leadership is the process of creating and communicating a vision that will inspire others to follow with commitment and enthusiasm. Employees are more likely to give wholehearted support to a leader when they feel this leader values them as individuals, actively seeks their opinions and makes them feel part of an organization with a vision shared by all its members.

> *Just as the intellect is the instrument of knowledge, so is the heart the instrument of inspiration.*

Essential to the understanding of this whole process is realizing that the key word is feel. People relate to people at the feeling level. Being analytical all the time makes us inaccessible, and people feel shut out. Managers who are in touch with and make use of their whole brain have a greater range of skills and approaches at their disposal.

Leadership is an extension of the total person, the analytical you and the feeling you — the truly and completely human you. To be the most effective leader, dare to be the most complete and balanced human being you can be. We become the complete human being we can be by celebrating life in its fullness — by leading a balanced life.

2.   Love and the Human Heart

We are social animals. We have a need to belong, to connect. Love helps us belong and connect to others. Love can be defined in many ways, but my favorite is the following definition. The basic minimum requirement of any loving relationship you are in is that the other person's happiness is as important to you as your happiness. The complete requirement for developing a deeper relationship is that the other person's happiness is more important to you than your own.

Under this definition, it is not just sufficient to just say "I love you." It has to be reflected in our daily behavior, in our allocation of time and energy — being there at children's soccer games and piano recitals, sharing our significant other's interests. When needs of the heart are met, it sings and makes us a more complete and effective person and thus a better leader.

Commenting on American Express CEO James Robinson in the January 24, 1988, issue of Business Week, Henry Kissinger, an American Express director, is quoted as saying: "Linda [Robinson's wife] has given him a human dimension that's made him a lot more attractive."

Robinson agreed: "Linda's into talking about feelings, and I've learned to do more of it. My relationship with my kids has never been better, and that's largely because of Linda." Expression of feelings is an integral part of establishing intimacy.

To tap the discretionary effort in the organization, the leader has to appeal not just to the mind but to the heart as well. The following unwritten employment contract with the new breed of workers emphasizes this relationship.

> **Level I contribution:** I need a job to pay for my basic needs (fulfilling the needs of the body). You give me a job, and I will give you just enough to keep my job.

> **Level II contribution:** If the job is interesting and challenging (fulfilling the needs of the mind in addition to

meeting the basic needs), then I will give to the job much more than the minimum daily requirement.

Level III contribution: If the job, the organization, and the manager make me feel valued as a person with a life outside the job and provide a sense of meaning and contribution to the community at large (fulfilling the needs of the spirit, mind and body), then I will give you all I have to offer — esprit de corps.

3.   Interpersonal and Intrapersonal

People who are preoccupied with themselves pay only superficial attention to other people. They are so tied up in themselves that they cannot observe the subtleties in another person's feelings, nor can they really listen. As a result, they cannot really respond to other people as individuals. They talk past the other person, never really connecting in an authentic way.

We cannot give to people what we don't have. As managers, we need to make people feel at ease in their relationship with us so they will feel comfortable in sharing "bad news." If we are not at ease with ourselves, then we cannot make others feel at ease. Withholding "bad news" gives a manager an incomplete picture of the realities the organization faces, which results in less than optimum decisions.

We cannot give to people what we don't have. If we are not at ease with ourselves, then we cannot make others feel at ease.

We try to compartmentalize our life as working professional/manager, father/mother, golfer/gardener, etc. The whole person comes to work, however, and, as you saw in Chapter III, each part of the multi-dimensional self impacts the others. If we are not patient with ourselves, then we can not be patient with others.

4.   Know and Feel

He begins by asking, 'Is management in reality a rational task performed by rational people according to sensible organizational objectives?' We all know better, yet the myth of rationality persists in spite of all evidence to the contrary. Much of our society and most of our business life is organized around airtight logic, numbers, and explanations that "make sense." However, a whole range of logic-defying emotions — rage, fear, insecurity, jealousy, and passion — are acted out in the office. It is these powerful yet unacknowledged feelings that often disrupt our organization.

Most executives have a notoriously underdeveloped capacity for understanding and dealing with emotions. All but the best are reluctant to ask themselves why they act the way they do. As a result, most fail to understand both their own managerial behavior and that of others.

— Harry Levinson in Jan./Feb. 1996 *Harvard Business Review*, reviewing the book *Life and Death in the Executive Fast Lane* by Manfred F.R. Kets de Vries

What makes us human is our capacity to feel, and to think about our purpose in life, and to make choices that lead us to our purpose. We know and have seen that when employees feel motivated, they produce more and give better customer service. To the contrary, if the employees feel demotivated, their performance is subpar. We've all seen a less-talented basketball team beat a more-talented team because the less-talented players were more motivated.

We need to recognize that feelings do exist in the managerial and executive suites as well. Once we recognize this fact, then our goal becomes very clear: Maximize the positive feelings and thus the positive contributions from self and others in the organization and successfully deal with the negative feelings and distractions. Relationships between the manager and the employees based on fear are not conducive to the sharing of creative ideas and implementing of changes.

The following quote illustrates well the role of feelings in implementing new ways of doing business.

To think that resistance won't occur or to view those who

exhibit its symptoms as difficult or retrograde is a fatal mistake .... The real cause of reengineering failure is not the resistance itself but management's failure to deal with it ... Achieving real change means responding to the stuff — including powerful emotions like fear and anger — that drives real human beings' behavior in real jobs.

— Michael Hammer in *Fortune*, April 17, 1995

5.   Inner Security

It does not matter what field of work we are in, circumstances are changing fast. Technology, especially the application of computer technology, has resulted in significant advancements in both the service and the manufacturing sectors. The knowledge base acquired in college is no longer adequate preparation for a career. More time must be devoted to keeping up with the advancements in one's field. Otherwise, insecurity may set in.

By drawing life fulfillment from supportive relationships, leisure activities and spiritual growth, we don't put all our eggs in the "career" basket. If we look for all of our life fulfillment from our business career then we put too much pressure on this one aspect of life. We can't afford for anything to go wrong in our career, and this leads to not fully trusting others — especially if their role can have an impact on how our performance is judged.

Spiritual growth helps us develop faith in our own capabilities, and thus we learn to trust ourselves. This leads us into trusting the goodwill of others to make right choices and act responsibly. .

We know that to be successful in our career, we need to work hard but that often means taking our personal relationships for granted. Without constant attention, once supportive relationships can become non-supportive. As a tiny, delicate flower in sufficient numbers can color a hillside, small pleasures and rewards can add up to fulfillment if repeated often enough. The three most effective resources for stress management — relationships, recreation and religion — are also the same resources for inner security.

6.   Being at Peace

When we are at peace internally, our demeanor externally is calm. We don't have this need to be right or to have the right answer to every problem. When we feel we have the right answer, we stop looking for new information. In other words, we stop listening and thus stifle creativity in the organization.

To be at peace, we have to be attuned to our feelings and needs. Just as a tight shoe conveys the message that it is too tight, feelings of restlessness and boredom convey to us that needs are going unmet in one or more areas of our life. People who cannot find time for recreation are obliged sooner or later to find time for illness.

When we are at peace, we have access to all of our mental resources, both analytical and intuitive. Einstein himself said, "I never discovered anything with my rational mind."

7.   Creativity in Action

As professionals and managers, our effectiveness is measured by the creativity of our decisions. We're paid for the quality of our decisions and not for the number of hours spent at the desk. All thinking and decision making is done in the mind. Therefore, to understand the creative process, we need to understand the mind — its makeup and functioning.

Creative decision making in the business world is seeing the bigger picture, the connections between seemingly unrelated variables, the possibilities and putting the pieces together. These creative and intuitive processes call upon the right side of our brain — the intuitive side— more so than the left side.

Any activity that helps us develop the right brain in essence helps us develop our creative potential. The leisure pursuits of music, drawing, reading, writing, painting, etc., help develop the right hemisphere of the brain. So when we take time to engage in our hobbies and/or leisure activities, we are not just recharging our batteries physically but also developing our creative potential.

The mind is like a huge computer that stores and processes endless amounts of information. The more experiences we have, the more we have from which to draw. Often, creative solutions come from looking for ideas in a completely unrelated field. Leisure and self-actualization activities provide experiences in unrelated fields and help to unleash the intuitive, creative, holistic side of the brain.

We have all experienced that when we are angry, we can't think straight because we lose part of our thinking power. An unbalanced life, over time, can create an inner conflict that may be invisible to others who only see our outer material and career success. This type of conflict does not allow us to form a complete picture of the problem we're trying to address. Hence, the solution we come up with is not as creative because it is based on an incomplete picture. When the mind is agitated, the power of intellectual discrimination is diminished.

8. Energy and an Unbalanced Life

We have all experienced days when we were full of energy, as well as days when we were constantly tired. On some of the days when we felt tired, it was not the result of doing any more physical work. It was simply because of the presence of one or more energy-absorbing feelings, such as a conflict with a supervisor, colleague or subordinate.

The inner needs don't go away just because we're too busy in meeting career needs. If ignored, inner needs create internal conflict. People with inner conflict spend huge amounts of energy in dealing with internal anxieties.

A healthy body provides physical energy. A healthy mind provides mental and emotional energy. A healthy spirit provides spiritual energy. Energy flow from within can be blocked by many things, including pride and selfishness.

> If you want to manage somebody, manage yourself. Do that well and you'll be ready to start managing and start leading.
> — From *Leaders: The Strategies for Taking Charge*
> by Warren Bennis and Burt Nanus

9. In Harmony

Cooperation requires listening to others and being supportive of other team members without any concern as to who gets the credit. Being in harmony with oneself results in an expanded definition of the self, which has no need for taking credit. External rewards, while welcome, are not that important. The focus becomes doing one's part and believing that if the team is successful, then rewards will follow.

A hierarchical position has a built-in wall to open communication from subordinates. The manager needs to be aware of this reality, and on an ongoing basis has to make an extensive effort to break down those barriers. If the personal ego comes into play, this wall becomes even higher. A person with an unchecked ego is forced to think and behave as follows:

- I'm the boss and must have answers to every problem.
- If the idea is not mine, it is not good.

In this state, when somebody disagrees with our chain of thought and ideas, our ego processes it as a threat to our self esteem. We become defensive, and when we're defensive, we resort 100 percent to the analytical half and block the creative half. We may even become vicious and emotionally negative.

On the other hand, a manager who is in harmony with himself understands that creative leadership is not having the right answer to every problem. It is asking the right question that leads the other team members to the right solution.

> The way a team plays as a whole determines its success. You may have the greatest bunch of individual stars in the world, but if they don't play together, the club won't be worth a dime.
>
> — Babe Ruth

Management is a team sport. Each department has to work with every other department to make sure products and services are delivered on time. By his example, the manager sets the tone for the whole department.

10. Reflection and Learning

Reflection is the processing of personal life experiences to learn, among other things, which activities, thought processes and behaviors helped us grow and experience happiness, and which produced the opposite results. With reflection, we can achieve a greater and deeper level of self knowledge. Without a reflective temperament, long life means only long existence, nothing more. We just keep repeating the first round of experience.

By not processing our life experiences, we miss out on clarifying for ourselves what is important to us. The successful transformation to a more productive and fulfilling life must start from inside out. If you merely change your behavior temporarily, and your thoughts and belief systems stay the same, then the change will be very short lived.

> *Without a reflective temperament, long life means only long existence, nothing more. We just keep repeating the first round of experience.*

A successful balanced-life reclamation process starts inside out. Reflection will tell us that life is a process and not a project. Life has to be lived and enjoyed today, not put on hold until the annual vacation or the big promotion.

In today's fast changing, global economy, we have to learn from our experiences, both successes and failures, to stay effective on and off the job.

Mainstream corporations such as AT&T, PepsiCo, Hoechst Celanese, and Aetna are integrating various forms of introspection training into management development programs ... One evangelist is Joseph Galerneau, head of executive training at AT&T. His challenge is to try to transform a corps of disciplined order-followers into self-starting entrepreneurs. To that end, he devotes roughly one-fifth of his $3.5 million annual budget to courses that encourage introspection. "This company is not going to be successful unless we have people who can learn from experience."

— Stratford Sherman
in *Fortune*, August 22, 1994

11. Two Kinds of Education

Based on my observations over the past 20 years in the corporate world, I have often wondered how come so many "successful" people in their profession are not so successful in their personal life. The conclusion I have reached is that learning how to make a living and learning how to live are two distinct skill sets. The second education — learning how to live a meaningful and fulfilling life — we have to give ourselves.

We want to have a balanced and healthy lifestyle, but we do not know how because we are not born with the secret of how to live. Living a meaningful and fulfilling life in the modern world requires skills that our parents and even some of our mentors did not have or need to have. To develop balanced-life skills requires that we be willing to be introspective, to be patient with ourselves, to experiment, and to make a commitment to continuously update our skills and knowledge.

The pace of life in our age is much faster. We are trying to do more and more in less and less time. One fact that is so obvious, but which we often forget in the haste of our modern life, is that the clock does not stop ticking for anyone. Our children are growing up. We cannot postpone sharing their life and spending time with them.

> My husband never took time to understand their school problems or personal problems when they were little, and when it meant a lot for Dad to care. Now they don't come to him and he feels hurt and angry. He says he has given them so much and they are ungrateful. They really aren't ungrateful. They just don't feel they can really talk with him now.
> — A wife in her 50s in a *Wall Street Journal* series, "Executives' Wives Describe Effects of Husbands' Careers on Children," by Frank Allen

In the 1996 Atlanta Olympics, Hoyer-Larson of Denmark became the only non-Asian player to win a badminton medal in men's singles. He credits his improved game to the birth of his son the preceding year. "Knowing that badminton is not the most important thing in your life made me more relaxed on the court and I have become a better badminton player," he said. What this shows is that a healthy personal life, in fact, enhances job performance, and vice versa.

During the Leadership and Balanced Life seminars, participants often say, "I agree with what you are saying, and I want to lead a balanced life, but the world of work says 'Give me 16 hours,' and the whole thing breaks down."

Because the root causes of the breakdown are both within us and outside of us, the solution therefore lies both within and without. As professionals and managers, our effectiveness is measured by the creativity of our decisions and our leadership skills. We are paid for the quality of our decisions and not for the number of hours spent at the desk.

Proper understanding of the 11 principles and practices will give you the internal strength to start addressing this breakdown. Once you internalize these principles, then you will be able to see that the best thing you can do to enhance the quality of your job performance is to make time for yourself.

The quality of your life and the quality of work are mutually supportive. This point was made in a 1996 *Fortune* study. It clearly indicated that the best, most productive employees are those who have a life outside the office.

Armed with this new awareness, you will be able to give yourself permission to reduce the number of 16-hour work days. Once you internalize these principles, you will be able to say to yourself, "When I am taking time out to lead a balanced life, I am not short-changing my career or the organization, but in fact, I am developing and unleashing my creativity and leadership potential."

When we repeatedly give this message to the mind, it can assist us in finding solutions to the bulging in-basket and meeting-overload phenomenon. This is how the commercials on television work: remind and reinforce.

Information in this book will help you restore balance and pleasure to your life, and as a byproduct help you unleash your leadership and creativity. If you burn the candle at both ends, you can be more effective in the short term, but you will burn out and be less effective in the long run.

In his book, *Time Shifting: Creating More Time to Enjoy Your Life*, Stephen Rechtschaffen, M.D., points out that constant rushing robs us of peace of mind and basic pleasures that are our birthright. Further, a life of frantic activity denies us the time for meaningful communication with others, leisurely meals, play and laughter, relaxed and comfortable time with ourselves and the ability to experience the beauty of life all around us.

There are many new and not-so-new management practices and strategies for improving competitive advantage and profitability, such as Total Quality Management, Process Reengineering, Strategic Alliances, etc. None of these strategies are applicable to all situations. Just because one may have produced excellent results in another company does not mean that it will produce similar results in your company.

There are many variables that must be considered in adapting or modifying any one strategy, such as your core competencies, products and services, level of technology, competitive environment, customer profile, etc.

What is required is a personalized and creative solution that takes into account the specifics of your environment. The people in the organization are in the best position to come up with these creative solutions. The more access decision makers in the organization have to their creativity, the more creative their solutions will be.

Unmet inner needs act like a dam on the flow of creativity. Applied creativity is an an extension of the inner self. A balanced life meeting the needs of the multi-dimensional inner self is the key to unleashing creativity.

The success of any organization ultimately depends on the *quality* of the decisions made by every employee every day. Therefore, it is in the manager's interest that his primary mission be creating an environment that allows him and others in the organization to lead balanced lives for unleashing creativity and making quality decisions every day.

6

Leadership Behaviors for Tapping Discretionary Effort

THERE IS ENORMOUS UNTAPPED POTENTIAL found in the employees of most large organizations. The ability to tap the latent commitment, enthusiasm and creativity of everyone in an organization is demonstrably the one unifying theme found in the achievements of all great organizations. The manager's behavior plays a key role in tapping this discretionary effort.

Within the highly competitive globalized marketplace, corporations can no longer increase prices at will to increase profits. Under this scenario, the only way to increase profits is to reduce operating costs. To reduce operating costs, things must be done differently.

Inflation alone will increase operating costs when a business fails to change and continues to do things the way they have always been done. In other words, corporate management practices must change. Corporations must become innovative to survive, let alone succeed.

Innovation does not just happen. It must be actively supported and managed. Individual employee creativity is the source of innovation. Managers have to create an environment where employees feel comfortable in suggesting and experimenting with new ways of doing things.

Management of practical innovation requires leadership skills and an understanding of what makes people tick. Leaders do not control — they enable others to act.

> *Employees throughout the organization must feel an ownership and personal responsibility for the customer, the service and the product.*

Most frontline managers are in their current positions because of technical skills or discrete product knowledge. They are trained to control outcomes. They were excellent individual contributors before being promoted to the frontline manager position. However, technical skills do not prepare one for inspiring people or leading behavioral changes.

Employees throughout the organization must feel an ownership and personal responsibility for the customer, the service and the product. Upper management observes the $10-million problems, but sees very few of the $10 problems.

The $10 problems can only be solved by individuals at every level of an organization who care. Attention to this type of detail by everyone is the way corporations can nurture innovation, continue to experience growth and improve profit margins.

Following are charts that illustrate how a leader prompts positive employee motivation in particular management situations. Questions were asked of the employees as to what makes them give that extra 40 percent — the discretionary effort — in the form of enthusiasm, commitment and creativity to the job and company.

When Managers:	Employee Enthusiasm Results When:
1. Talk face-to-face about the contribution the individual and department make, and share the results.	1. I feel I am making a difference. I can see the results of my effort — the finished product.
2. Look for what is going right, and provide personalized positive feedback. Take into consideration other's feelings.	2. I am appreciated/rewarded for my efforts.
3. Set up work objectives that inspire. Because of span-of-control goals resulting in fewer management positions and reduced upward mobility, help employees expand the definition of success.	3. I am doing something that I enjoy and also provides an opportunity to grow/self-actualize.

When Managers:	Employee Commitment Results When:
1. Translate corporate vision for the department and share with the group a mental picture — not of what we are, but of what we need to be.	1. I feel I am part of a winning team that is going places.
2. Involve others by actively soliciting solutions to problems.	2. I have a say in how we go about doing our jobs.
3. Regularly repeat the contribution that the company's product and service make to society and mankind.	3. I believe in the value of the end product (its contribution to society at large).

When Managers:	Employee Innovation Results When:
1. Change their paradigm from viewing employees as a set of hands to viewing them as a source of ideas. Regularly ask employees what specific changes they have made lately.	1. The corporate culture expects and supports change.
2. Allow time to think and listen.	2. I have time to think, and when my ideas are listened to.
3. Help employees enhance their self-esteem by making them feel important. Create an environment that encourages people to experiment and take risks.	3. I feel secure to suggest new ways of doing things and to take risks.

What has been illustrated on the previous pages is nothing new to the manager who has been keeping abreast of current trends in managing for productivity. Intellectually, most managers understand what must be done and how one should behave to be an effective leader.

Then why, when employees were surveyed as to the greatest need for employee training, was "getting along with difficult people" the top priority in an organization that prides itself in building "community"? Something is missing. Managers need help.

An employee of a Fortune 500 company tells the story of one of the vice-presidents, after having read Kenneth Blanchard and Spencer Johnson's *One Minute Manager*, talking at length to his staff and strongly recommending that everyone get a copy of the book.

One of the main messages in the book calls for managers to catch their people doing things right and give them "one-minute praising." No one in this vice-president's department could ever recall being praised by him.

There are two primary reasons why we don't see leadership behavior in action on a day-to-day basis: lack of balance on the job and a lack of balanced life in general.

Lack of Balance on the Job

When an executive does not balance the time spent on technical, managerial and leadership tasks, there will be trouble. This is not an easy assignment, when an executive is required to call upon a combination of technical, managerial and leadership skills in successfully fulfilling his or her role.

Leadership tasks usually take the third priority behind technical and managerial tasks. One's "in basket" never gets empty, thus there never seems to be time for just talking with employees person to person. Leadership behavior, which builds medium- to long-term benefits, does not give the instant payoff or immediate sense of accomplishment that solving a knotty technical problem provides. Thus, one looking for instant reward will take the path of least resistance and do more managing of things rather than developing of people.

Lack of Balance off the Job (Balanced Life)

Even when we have a fairly optimum balanced life, and we function well on the job at one stage of our life, we must realize that as we grow and change in our job while also growing chronologically older, our personal needs change as well. Such change can be extraordinarily disruptive and — unless understood as a natural part of human development — potentially destructive.

Many times, we are not prepared for how these unperceived changes affect our commitments to particular relationships, career goals, and chosen lifestyles. Such change most certainly creates tension within ourselves and with others.

As we assume more responsibilities at work or in our personal lives, our needs and goals compete for the limited personal resources of time and energy, and conflict with each other as well as with the reality of the outside world. Psychological studies have shown the primary source of the dilemmas that leaders face is their own inner conflicts.

To lead successfully presupposes having much of one's own psychological house in order. It becomes a tough balancing act. These unpleasant feelings have to be dealt with, because if ignored, they don't just go away. Suppressed feelings develop into compensating behaviors that are not conducive to effective leadership.

Leadership Behavior to Tap Employee <u>Enthusiasm</u>	'Dam' Created by Unresolved Balanced-Life Concerns
1. Talk face-to-face about the contribution the individual and the department make, and share the results. Realize that as the corporation and the number of employees grow, jobs become specialized, and people tend to minimize their contribution.	1. Because of ignoring personal feelings, the manager tends to favor the rational/analytical side of her or his brain. Therefore, activity not involving rational/analytical skills is not appealing, and is seen as a waste of time.
2. Look for what is going right, and provide personalized positive feedback. Take into consideration others' feelings.	2. Even with achievements visible to the outside world, the manager doesn't feel fulfilled. This is the result of neglecting the needs of his or her multi-dimensional self. It is very hard to see the good in others unless one feels good about herself or himself.
3. Set up work objectives that inspire. Because of span-of-control goals resulting in fewer management positions and reduced upward mobility, help employees expand the definition of success.	3. Through the tendency to be totally dependent on work for all of life's kicks, the delegation skill — though intellectually understood — is practiced selectively. Managers tend to think: "This report is going to the senior officers of the company, so I must do the report myself." This operating mode denies growth opportunities for subordinates and shortchanges the company.

Leadership Behavior to Tap Employee <u>Commitment</u>	'Dam' Created by Unresolved Balanced-Life Concerns
1. Translate corporate vision for the department and share with the group. Vision is a mental picture not of what we are, but of what we need to be. How are we going to get from here to there? Shared vision molds individuals into a common direction. The leader has to almost be evangelical about it.	1. "Busy Executive" driven by the need to control is so tied up in the day-to-day details that he or she does not have time for stepping back and conceptualizing the bigger picture — developing a vision. Before a manager can expect his vision to be shared by subordinates, he needs to *have* a vision.
2. Involve others by actively soliciting solutions to problems.	2. Unresolved career and personal concerns create inner tension, which interferes with a person's ability to integrate and use information — the most important step in problem solving and decision making.
3. Employees need to hear, again and again, the value of the end product and its contribution to society at large.	3. Again, unless the manager makes it a high priority in his or her mind, and on her or his schedule, it will be superseded by other, "more urgent" activities.

Leadership Behavior to Tap Employee <u>Creativity</u>	'Dam' Created by Unresolved Balanced-Life Concerns
1. Change your paradigm from viewing employees as a set of hands to viewing them as a source of ideas. Allow time to think and listen.	1. People who are preoccupied with themselves pay only superficial attention to other people. They are so tied up in themselves that they cannot observe the subtleties in another person's feelings, nor can they really listen. As a result, they can not really respond to other people as individuals.
2. Help employees enhance their self-esteem by creating an environment that encourages people to experiment and take risks.	2. Because of a manager's low frustration tolerance, subordinates are afraid to voice their opinions. Relationships based on fear are not healthy or conducive to spontaneity and enhancing self-esteem.
3. Expect employees to innovate by regularly asking them what specific changes they have made lately.	3. If a manager is insecure and fears failure, he or she will not take the risk involved in starting new projects and exploring new ways of doing things. She or he will block the organization's creative potential for developing and implementing innovative solutions.

For too many years, we have treated employee development, work satisfaction and job motivation as if they existed apart from the fullness and richness of an employee's life. The reality is that employees do not live neat, compartmentalized lives in which each separate concern operates within a closed system.

In fact, off-the-job concerns affect the employee on the job and vice versa. An employee's psychological well-being and his or her work effectiveness go hand-in-hand.

An employee does not come to work at 8 a.m. and turn on a switch and say, "I'm at work, so I will just forget everything else going on in my life." She or he comes to work as a whole person, and unresolved personal conflicts are present even if they are not acknowledged.

Gary Trudeau, in a recent segment of *Doonesbury* comic strip, depicted the character Mike's inner voice protesting against the structures of his job, his marriage and his life in general. With comic-strip eloquence, he gave voice to the dissatisfaction many of the best and the brightest have with life on the managerial-corporate tract.

Increasingly, Baby Boomers, after achieving career success and affluence, are asking, "Is this all there is?" They are searching for guidance and ways to lead a balanced life — to enjoy their hard-earned success.

They are questioning heretofore accepted definitions of "the good life." They are asking if one can balance personal needs and career demands — very fundamental questions about where their life is going. The luster of the big paycheck may be dimming as individuals seek to redefine the "the good life."

This questioning cannot be ignored by management. In fact, many in management are the ones asking the questions. Is corporate America coming unglued? Individuals, managers with good jobs, are present at their desk but their heart — their drive — is in neutral, causing a pervasive malaise throughout the workplace.

These concerns have tremendous implications for business success in the coming decade. The success of a business depends on the people within the organization. If the heart, the passion and the focus of a person is not involved in his or her job, the organization suffers.

The competitive edge rests with the companies who retain the best management resources to achieve their corporate goals. The new breed of managers are different than their predecessors. The economic manager is being superseded by the psychological manager — managers for whom what Maslow called "the higher needs" have become important.

With the material needs satisfied, the need for challenging and significant work, for fulfilling relationships, and for a stimulating and fulfilling life experience become the prime motivating factor. When these needs are not met, frustration sets in.

Organizations that cannot respond to their employees as total human beings will stagnate and become less efficient than those organizations better able to assist their managers in successfully achieving both their career and personal balanced-life goals.

It is abundantly clear that personal off-the-job concerns do affect the manager on the job. Therefore, neither the corporation nor the manager can continue to look at work and career in isolation from other aspects of the manager's life.

Because the growth and productivity of organizations is more than ever dependent on the effectiveness of human performance, the corporations who choose to ignore this vital issue do so at a great cost to themselves.

When the people in the organization grow, the organization grows. It is in the organization's self-interest to help employees lead a balanced lifestyle.

Finally, in the 21st Century, the Return on Investment — the bottom line measurement — will be directly related to:

- Return on Ideas and Innovation,
- Return on Initiative
- Return on Interpersonal Relationships

The Ideas, Initiative and Interpersonal returns from leadership are byproducts of a work force that is able to access all of its inner resources.

7

People Self: The Total Self's Most Fulfilling Part and the Key to People Skills

If we have no peace, it is because we have forgotten that we belong to each other.

— Mother Teresa

THE RESULTS FROM LEADERSHIP and Balanced Life Seminars have confirmed what many studies have found about how people rank their values. People rank their top four life values as follows:

1. Family/Friends (People)
2. Inner Peace/Harmony (Actualization)
3. Health (Leisure)
4. Work (Career)

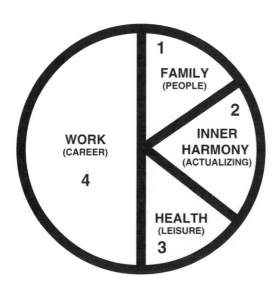

When people have a chance to reflect on what is really important, the career ranks fourth. But in practice, the career usually gets the largest allocation of time and energy.

The purpose of this chapter is to show how the four components of the Balanced Life Model can complement and enhance each other, rather than compete among themselves for our precious time.

PEOPLE SELF AND CAREER SELF: Conflict or Complement?

The career self satisfies some very important human needs:

1. The need to be somebody: The position on the corporate ladder, the title, professional success — all help meet this need.

2. The need to grow: By solving problems and successfully dealing with the challenges, we experience growth.

3. The need for material gain: We seek basic human necessities, as well as the luxuries we want.

4. The need for self-expression: Work and career provide the opportunity to express ourselves.

5. The need for accomplishment: We gain a sense of achievement as we complete assignments and projects.

Because of lopsided positive reinforcements on career and material success from the people around us and society in general, there is a seductive quality in career success.

To be a success in our work life, we all very clearly understand that we are to be creative and imaginative. To get that next promotion or merit increase, we need to show our superiors that we have something more to offer than our peers.

But in our relationships, as time goes by, we become unimaginative and dull. In other words, we give up our silly and playful ideas as years go by, when in fact, we need to be more imaginative to keep the romance and creativity alive.

As we achieve greater success in our careers, the increasing demands leave less time for personal life — People, Actualization and Leisure. Another more subtle change takes place that also works against the needs of the People Self. As we become more successful and more powerful, the people in our work life defer to us. When we get home, we expect the people at home to defer also, thus creating a barrier to spontaneity — the key to having fun.

In a healthy relationship, both partners come with an equal expectation of respect and consideration — not more and not less. Building a relationship requires admitting occasionally that you can be wrong. I've noticed, however, that as people become more successful, it becomes harder to accept and acknowledge that they are wrong.

We cannot postpone the balanced lifestyle until sometime in the future. The People Self has to be attended every day, every week and every month— especially when the children are young. How many times we've heard or said to ourselves, "Children grow up so fast."

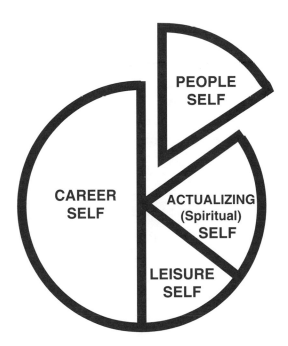

So much time is devoted to career — the fourth highest value — that we experience conflict between the work life and the personal life — the top three life values. When we tend to the needs of just one part of our self/life, we think the career and personal life are in conflict with each other.

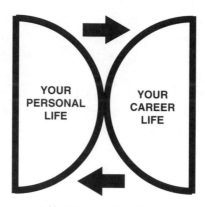

Life Viewed in Parts

Once we realize that we are whole persons and look at the totality of life, it becomes clear that we need all the pieces to be happy. Yes, the conflict will continue between the work life and personal life as long as we continue to look at needs of each self separately in terms of hours: "I can make one more sales call or attend one more meeting if I can spend just four more hours." This is the quantitative view.

It becomes easier to resolve this conflict once we shift the focus from quantity to the quality of life, to the whole life and not just the work life. The quality-of-life picture says, "Hey, the corporation won't go out of business if I take time to be with my family and friends."

This allows the number-one life value to take priority over the number-four life value. Work stress does not impact family life as much as problems at home impact the work performance.

Life Viewed as Whole

It took me a long time to learn what is really valuable in life. I went through a period of real acquisitiveness — buy this, buy that, get the most expensive car. Hell, get two of them! All these things, as if owning lots of stuff said a damn about who you really are and what your life really means.

Maybe I've finally learned what happiness is: my family, my wife, my kids. I've learned what my Dad tried to show me by how he lived — what's important and what's not. We're only here a short time. Let's enjoy it, whatever happens. Listen, everyday I'm thankful. The kids are well. We love each other. That's all that matters.

— John Candy
In *Parade* Magazine interview
May 3, 1992

The People Self and Other People

Balanced life and relationships also may be viewed in either a holistic or a conflictual way. Spouses and children can become just another demand on our time, or they can be the energy that keeps us going.

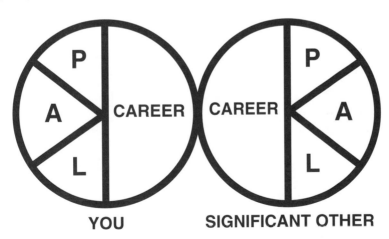

When we change the focus from self interests to common interests, the conflict goes away. Each partner's People Self needs can only be met by another person. Family relationships are critical in helping an individual to satisfy the relationship needs of the People Self. Developing a relationship requires looking at the needs of both persons in a mutual way rather than a competitive way. This approach allows relationships to energize rather than deplete each person.

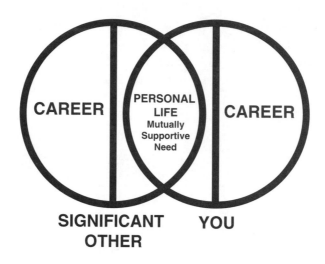

The great danger for family life, in the midst of any society whose idols are pleasure, comfort and independence, lies in the fact that people close their hearts and become self-ish. The fear of making permanent commitments can change the mutual love of husband and wife into two loves of self — two loves existing side by side until they end in separation ... Each one must show concern, not only for his or her own life but also for the lives of other members of the family: their needs, their hopes, their ideals.

— Pope John Paul II,
During 1979 visit to America
(As reported in *Parade* Magazine, May 3, 1992)

Self needs and common needs stop being in conflict once we look at our total needs. We are social animals, and we need people in our lives. The primary purpose of the thousands of clubs, associations and groups in this country is to bring together people with common interests.

The obligations to ourselves and to a larger entity, whether that is a relationship or a community, are not really in conflict. When we tend to a relationship, we in fact are tending to the People part of our Self. This understanding makes it easier to say "no" to requests that interfere with the balanced life.

Recently, the board of directors of the India Cultural Center organized a fundraising dinner. The author has been on the board for 10 years and has supported the project. However, the dinner was on Friday night, so I had to decline the invitation because it would have interfered with a planned family activity.

That night, my daughter, wife and I went out for a leisurely dinner at a new Italian restaurant in town. Had I gone to the fundraising dinner, I would have missed out on listening to my daughter tell about her chemistry experiment, her child development class's visit to St. Francis Hospital's maternity ward and her latest book report. The icing on the cake that evening was being able to watch with my family as the University of Memphis basketball team got its first win of the season after three disappointing losses — a perfect evening!

The happiest memories I have from my childhood are the annual family activities — the food, the laughs, the worship, the music. Rituals and traditions are extremely important. They provide continuity to the family experience and bring the family together as a unit. They meet the most important need of some consistency in this ever changing world, and they are also just pure fun!

No matter what, there are 8-10 activities/rituals/traditions that my own family makes sure take place every year: birthdays, anniversary, festivals from India, Thanksgiving, Christmas with my wife's brother's family, a Valentine party at home with friends, a Super Bowl party and a family vacation.

As we have experienced, the People Self is satisfied when we connect with others. To deal with the feelings of loneliness, we develop relationships. One People Self connects with another People Self through this wonderful feeling called love.

Like you, I've set goals, and after achieving some of them, have set higher goals. One of my top goals is to lead a balanced life today — not next month or next year or five years from now.

The People Self and the Spiritual Self

We are also a part of this wonderful and beautiful Creation. Our spiritual/actualizing self feels at peace when we connect with other beings and things in the Creation:

- Another human being — significant other
- A group of human beings — family, friends
- An even larger group — the community we live in
- The world we live in — people from other countries or cultures
- Pets, animals
- Growing things: plants, flowers, etc.
- Nature: woods, mountains, streams, lakes, ocean, etc.
- Inner self
- Higher Power

In her insightful book on the spiritual development of children, *Something More*, Jean Grasso Fitzpatrick, reminds us that spirituality has many faces. One of the faces of spirituality is that of a child.

The co-author was reminded of this wisdom recently when, during a particularly trying week at work, her 8-year-old daughter greeted her each morning with, "Look, Mommy, it's another beautiful day!" After several weeks of rainy weather, the child had grown keenly aware of the gift of sunshine and blue skies. What a wonderful way to begin the day!

Cecilia, on the other hand, tended to begin each day with her mental "to-do" list. By taking a moment just to listen to her child, she not only strengthened that personal relationship, but received a valuable spiritual gift as well. Without that spiritual and relational focus, it is too easy for each day to become nothing more than a series of tasks to be done.

Personal relationships are also emphasized in many organized religions, as well as in other groups that focus on spiritual growth. It is no accident that in churches, synagogues, temples and mosques, people worship in groups supporting and nurturing one another's faith. In these contexts, personal growth and spiritual growth are seen as complementary and interrelated rather than as competitive processes. By focusing on our lives as wholes rather than just on each component separately, we too can experience our personal and spiritual needs as supportive of one another.

There is one type of personal relationship that is not compatible with personal and spiritual growth. Relationships that are described in the current popular jargon as "co-dependent" actually retard the growth and development of each person.

Co-dependent relationships are those in which one person essentially lives his or her life through that of another person, trying to manipulate, beg, coerce, protect or deceive another person into doing what is wanted:

- A parent who feels unable to say "no" to her children even when their demands are excessive and inappropriate.
- A husband who deceives his wife about financial problems in order to "protect" her.
- A young adult who chooses his spouse or career only to "please" his parents.

All of these people are in relationships that diminish rather than enhance mutual growth and development.

Fortunately, it is often not necessary to terminate a co-dependent relationship in order to change it into a healthier one. When parents begin, for example, to set healthy limits with their children, they are often amazed at the scope of the results. Consider Bob's story. As a newly-divorced single parent, it was necessary for him to ask his children to assume more responsibility at home and curtail some of their spending habits:

> The first few weeks really were not very pretty. When I began to expect regular help with household chores and limit trips to fast-food restaurants, I was tense and defensive, and the children were irritable and uncooperative. The whining was awful! The changes happened so slowly that I was not even aware of them. One Friday I came home from work to find that the kids had done extra chores and had even packed their suitcases and mine for the upcoming weekend trip!

The benefits of this changed relationship went far beyond the completion of household chores. No book, lecture or class on responsibility and family values could have taught Bob's children more than the experience they had within their own family of seeing first-hand how mutual respect works in real life.

If we could put their experiences into the balanced-life diagram, we would see how the healthy growth of the People Self in each person spread out like ripples on a pond to positively impact each of the other aspects of the whole person.

The People Self, Health and Leisure

One of the characteristics of the Balanced Life Model discussed earlier was that the four components of the Total Self are mutually supportive. The People Self helps in achieving and experiencing the third-ranked life value as well: health and leisure.

> A great deal of new research from Berkeley and other leading institutions indicates that the emotional support you receive from your closest relationships may be more valuable to your resistance to disease than any surgical innovation, medication, or mineral supplement on the market. Time and again, these new studies have shown that mortality and disease may be directly related to the stress of loneliness and isolation. As far as dealing with stress, the research shows that the once-popular song was right: The only way to get by is with the help of your friends.
>
> — From *Wellness Letter*,
> University of California, Berkeley

A balanced lifestyle does not just help you enjoy your life in the present, it also prepares you for a fulfilling and healthy retirement. A balanced life has allowed you to develop other interests and activities to take the place of full-time work. But most important, the People Self has helped you build a social-support system of people whom you care about and who care about you. As the following quote reflects, building deep relationships and friendships takes time — a long time.

> "Still — in a way — nobody sees a flower — really — it is so small — we haven't time — and to see takes time, like to have a friend takes time."
>
> — Georgia O'Keeffe

As we've discussed, relationships develop over time. It requires sharing of self — your time and energy doing things together, having fun, communicating and just being around to share each other's joys and sorrows.

The author did not think much about retirement up until this year. "Oh, retirement is for old people. I'm young," I would always say. "Now at 48, it does not seem that far away. It is hard to believe that I've been in the corporate world for 25 years. Fourteen years are not that long a time until age 62 when I would like to retire. Not just retire, period, but retire to an active professional as well as social life — a management counselor professionally and remaining active socially with supportive relationships.

The People Self and Self-Esteem

You may find yourself or another person busy finding faults with other people, or being mean to other people. It shows that the person who is being mean is unfulfilled. The person who is finding fault with others is insecure.

Instead of dealing with the unhappiness in his or her life in a healthy way, the person is masking his or her insecurity and unhappiness by putting other people down. Unfortunately there are people like that on the job as well as off the job.

There is not much you can do about the lack of fulfillment in the other person's life, but what you can do is to make sure that your own life is fulfilled. That way, the other person's fault-finding will not diminish your life.

When you're unfulfilled (not meeting each of the four Self needs), then you expect other people in your life to be perfect. The author can recall a time when I was not happy with my career, and I expected my wife and children to be perfect. I would come home and find reasons to get upset.

After I accepted the fact that I wasn't going to get a promotion every three years, I looked for other ways to experience growth. I started asking my boss for assignments outside my immediate area of responsibility. This move gave me the opportunity to learn more about Federal Express' operations and also gave the company a fresh point of view.

I enjoyed this excursion into the new area tremendously. It

provided the challenge I needed after being in the same function/department for 10 years. After about nine months of part-time work in that area, I was offered a lateral move to manage the new area. Being part of the strategic planning group, this job provides ample opportunity to be creative and to be challenged.

> Two points need to be noted here:
> **1.** The unresolved Career Self was impacting my People Self. Once I accepted that fact and took initiative to deal with those issues, it improved both the personal and career life.
> **2.** The second point is how I chose this option over the others. As most professionals do, I get calls from managerial/professional recruiters known as "head hunters." I had calls for jobs in other cities. Even though their offers met the Career Self's growth needs by providing new challenges and more money, the move would have negatively impacted my People Self. My wife had just gone back to school to get a degree in computer science, and my son was in his final year of high school. Of course, they would have moved if I had insisted, but it would not have been a happy move. The total self/life approach was the key to making this decision.

Once you know yourself better and accept yourself, you develop a high self-esteem. You also begin to accept others as they are, rather than trying to change them. People are different from one another, and that is what differentiates us from robots. We all have different software — the programs that control our behavior. When you understand this, then you can stop expecting people to behave exactly as you want them to.

When you do stop expecting from people what they cannot give, then you can enjoy what they do have to offer, and that is a lot! It comes as a shock to many of us to learn that other people are just as frustrated with us when we don't behave exactly as they expect!

Balanced Life and Sexual Relationships

The Balanced Life Model can also help deal with one of the not so uncommon behaviors that affect the People Self very negatively: affairs. Quite frequently we see on the news or read in the papers how successful people from all walks of life — business, politics, judiciary, academia, religion, etc. — have affairs in which they risk everything they have achieved professionally and personally.

When you do stop expecting from people what they cannot give, then you can enjoy what they do have to offer, and that is a lot!

Our physical bodies have needs and desires, including sexual ones. The Balanced Life Model recognizes and celebrates the fullness of life, including physical and sexual needs. We are physical beings as well as mental, spiritual, and emotional ones.

The problems occur when the physical needs and desires are in control of the whole picture to the neglect of the other needs and goals. The difference between humans and animals is the power of discrimination — the power to differentiate between what will help you achieve the goal of a fulfilling life and what will help you achieve satisfaction only in the present moment. The Balanced Life Model tells us that happiness and life fulfillment are by-products of a person's celebrating life in all its fullness. Once you truly understand that, then you can determine what helps you and what harms you in celebrating your own life in its fullness.

Sexual desire is very powerful, and if not controlled or directed, it can lead us to do things that are not in our own best interests. The Balanced Life Model raises the following questions regarding a sexual relationship or encounter:

1. For a one-night stand (or even for several nights), do I want to jeopardize my marriage and family — the People Self?

2. Do I really want to do anything that gets in the way of my spiritual growth — the Actualization Self?

By internalizing and asking these questions, we shift the focus from a unidimensional self (physical/sexual) to a multi-dimensional whole self and add the People and Spiritual selves to the decision-making process. This process is analogous to important decisions being made by the entire management team or executive committee, rather than by an individual acting on his or her own with only partial information.

It is the privilege of human beings to experience whole-life fulfillment. To enjoy life fulfillment, the body, mind and spirit have to exist in a proper relationship with each other. If we are not in physical, mental and spiritual harmony, then our minds become slaves to our desires. The mind stays preoccupied with sense gratifications and we lose our power of discrimination — the judgment to evaluate what is right and what is wrong.

What is right is what allows you to live at peace with yourself, the people around you and the community at large, and what allows you to experience a life of joy and completeness. There is no joy without peace of mind.

Is it easy? No! Is it worth it? You decide!

The Big Picture: The People Self and the Whole Self

I am sure you know people who appear to "have it all," and — in your view — are successful and happy. After spending time with some of the "have it all" individuals, however, a pattern often emerges.

After talking about the successful career, the material possessions and the active social life, invariably comments such as this come forth: "In other people's eyes, I have it all, but I often feel that something is missing."

What is missing is the real needs of the People Self and the Spiritual Self. The physical needs are being met, but the People Self wants meaningful and caring relationships, and the Whole Self demands balance.

Before the author's son made his college choice, father and son visited the University of Michigan campus at Ann Arbor. On the drive back to Memphis he asked me, "Dad, won't you have to sacrifice to be able to pay the out-of-state tuition and other expenses?"

"No," I replied, "I have already planned for this and have saved that money. There is nothing for you to worry about. One of the greatest joys of life for your mother and me is to help and watch you and your sister grow. Instead of a sacrifice, it is a joy to be able to help you realize your potential. A big part of my definition of success is helping you build a foundation for whatever you choose to achieve in life."

A major part of my own success was the four gifts given to me by my own parents:

1. Education
2. Belief in myself
3. Belief in the Creator and daily spiritual practices
4. A loving home where I always belong and can return

I would like to do my part in helping my own children to realize these too.

Once we remind ourselves of the total life values and priorities, it becomes easier to determine how the personal resources of time and money need to be allocated. It was of zero concern to me that in order to be able to set aside savings for the children's college expenses, I drove a noisy Volkswagen Rabbit Diesel for more than eight years.

In addition to not having to make car payments for six of those years, the Rabbit's 50 miles-per-gallon provided a dividend of about $50-per-month through reduced gas purchases.

I am sure you know that diesel cars are noisier than gasoline cars, but let me tell you, the older diesels are even louder! My colleagues at work would laugh and say, "Madan, we can hear you coming a half mile away." They also reminded me that as director of the department, my image called for a better car. Even my own kids would refuse to ride in my car, preferring their mom's newer station wagon. I just laughed with them. When someone who didn't know me would ask what I drove, I simply replied, "It's German and a diesel!"

Once our lifestyle reflects our inner values, the external pressures to conform can be handled without disturbing our balanced life. One good measure of how much you love someone is to see how much you are willing to give.

Look back on your own life experience and see if you, like so many others, will come to the conclusion reflected by the title of this chapter: People Self: The Total Self's Most Fulfilling Part and the Key to People Skills.

> I fooled myself into thinking I was indestructible. You're seeing a guy who just stared right into the abyss. Things I didn't think about too much are now important, and that's human relationships and the love of a lot of people and how valuable they are. Forget money and power ... I had no idea how wonderful people are. I wish I had known this before. What a way to find out ... This whole experience has taught me something new about love, family, and mankind in general.
>
> — Lee Atwater, GOP political advisor,
> while facing terminal illness.
> From interview with Columbia, S.C., newspaper

It is ironic that we learn most about life when facing serious illness. It doesn't have to be that way if we take time for reflection and introspection. It is a beautiful life. Let's celebrate it in its fullness today, this week, this month, this year!

8

The Balanced Life in Action: Conversations with Successful Individuals

I don't think much of a man who is not wiser today than he was yesterday.

— Abraham Lincoln

WHAT'S THE DIFFERENCE BETWEEN YESTERDAY and today that should make us wiser? What's the difference between last year and this year? What's the difference between now and five years ago?

One obvious difference is that we're one day, one year or five years older. This fact of getting older does not automatically make one wiser. But it does provide the raw material, the other difference in addition to being older: experience.

More specifically, life experience. It is the processing of this raw material to determine what is and is not really important in leading a fulfilling life that makes us wiser. Socrates also expressed similar sentiments when he said, "An unexamined life is not worth living."

This chapter will present conversations with various individuals reflecting on their life experiences. These individuals are successful in their chosen fields professionally, and at the same time have managed to lead balanced lives.

Conversation with Joel, Management Consultant

Joel is 47 years old and has been married for 24 years. He has two daughters, and both are in college.

Q: *If you were to define for yourself the ideal balanced life, how would you define that?*

A: I guess you would have to provide for all of those things for which you have a passion or emotion. There are a lot of things. On the personal side, a sense of companionship and love and family and a sense of building a good home for yourself and those that you care about. Then you have the other side. That's the personal-achievement side. The sense that everyone wants to be, as Andy Warhol says, famous for a few minutes in their lifetime. So there is an effort toward doing something that's recognized, publicly.

And then there's the side that says that you're making a contribution that will be left behind. For some reason, when you're no longer putting your footprints in the sand, someone will remember that you've been there. I think there needs to be time for contemplation and introspection, personal development. For me, it is driven by the things I really draw a lot of pleasure from. If one of those gets left out and I'm not finding time for it, I start to get restless. If something is not right, I begin to feel troubled about it.

Q: *So you feel restless when you cannot find time for one of your passions?*

A: Yes. The marketing term is "cognitive dissonance," I guess. Lots of times you'll feel something unsettling, and you don't know what it is. For example, the last few days I've had trouble staying focused on projects at work. You know, there is plenty to do but I feel I've been doing too much of it. I've just finished a project, so now I feel like I can give a little bit of time to something else and kind of reward myself for getting that done. Mentally, I could not leap right into another heavy project right now. I need to do some other things. This weekend I built some cabinets to store things in the garage. I had other things I needed to do, but I just did that. For me that was recreation — a little break. The other thing that is going on is my feeling a need for us as a family to get away and take some vacation time. We haven't done that in a while, and it's time for us to do that too.

Q: *Especially, with kids as old as mine and yours are, they don't want to spend that much time with parents anyway.*

A: That's right. Ours are just going off to college. They are both going to be gone this fall, and once they get in school, they are pretty well gone. We'd better get a little time in here before they get busy in their own stuff, so there is that going on too.

Q: *Could you recall some time when it was out of balance and what was causing it?*

A: It does happen. If there are a lot of family pressures — for example, when I have a houseful of company for two weeks, and I know that there are things at work that aren't getting done, I start to get real irritable. I lose my attention span and so forth. It happens both ways. To lots of folks it just happens at work, and that's probably the most common. It's the sense of responsibility you have, I guess. But it also happens when you start to feel imposed upon by anything, whether it's family or home.

Q: *So any imbalance can go either way?*

A: I remember we talked about priorities. My first job, after the military, I was working with a guy who was an avid golfer. Golf was a way of life with him on the weekend. I mean that's what he did. At that point, I was in my first job and still finding my way. I wasn't yet really sure of who I was in this world of work or what was going on. I thought, well, he's a fellow that I'm working for, and I kind of respect him, and that must be what you do. So I caught myself getting up at like 4:30 on Saturday morning to drive for a 6:18 tee time and playing terribly, being mad and hating every minute of it and going back and saying "Gee, wasn't that fun." It finally dawned on me that that wasn't fun at all. And besides that, talk about your "spouse balance" — I mean, that was out of whack, too. It was clear to me that she really resented my going and spending a half a day golfing and then being so tired the other half of the day that I couldn't even deal with anything that was going on. So I said, "Life's too short to do this."

Q: *And you were doing it because your boss played golf?*

A: Yes. I mean it wasn't something he was imposing upon me, but if you were going to be one of the guys in the business world, this is what you did. It took a while to sort that out. I still play terrible golf, but I enjoy it a lot more than I did back then because I don't take it so seriously.

Q: *How would you describe the "success" yardstick against which you measure yourself?*

A: Well, that's changed a lot. Up until a half a dozen years ago, I thought the economics were the way you keep score. When I was working in the corporate world, I was doing well. We were able to save quite a bit of money and we were making good money. Then, I made some discoveries about the corporate world and found out that maybe I wasn't really cut out to be there after all. I find being on my own much more personally satisfying. The consequence is I don't make as much money, so there is a trade-off. I would have to say I am happier making less money and making it the way I want.

> *I made some discoveries about the corporate world and found out that maybe I wasn't really cut out to be there after all. I find being on my own much more personally satisfying.*

Q: *We were talking about how the definition of the yardstick changes. Is it because you get older, or the life experiences, or what?*

A: Yes, no one ever lies on their deathbed and wishes they spent more time at the office. It just doesn't happen. I think the thing that has been most helpful for me probably is recognizing that I am what I am — that is that I am independent and prefer to be that way. Everything else is ... you collect a lot of stuff, as George Carlin says, but it's just stuff. If you lost everything tomorrow, you could always get another job, so it's not the end of the world. I guess it's a matter of putting all the material things that we tend to drive ourselves for into a little different perspective and enjoy them, sure, but it's not the meaning of life. You can get along without them.

Q: *You mentioned that you enjoy the work you do because it helps you to be more yourself. Is that one of the driving motivations?*

A: Yes, it is for me. If I were trapped in a situation in which I wasn't learning anything, just doing the same stuff, 35 years of doing one-year stuff, I just couldn't do that. For me, it is very important to keep learning and listening. That's why I like spending time with different people, because you always learn something in what's going on with them. I really value that. I try to encourage our daughters to do that too, and Sue as well, to be curious and to be open-minded and to really try to discover things and to observe and pay attention. I look back on my high school, or even through college, and I wasted a lot of time. This really troubles me now because now I pay attention to what's going on — to what's happening.

I think it's typical of a kid — you go through life and all of a sudden you wake up and you say "What did I do?" You were just kind of there. You were just kind of average, or at least I was. I was really kind of in the middle of the pack. I had a good time, but I can't look back and say this was really great or I really learned a lot from this or that or whatever. You talk about regrets. What I regret is not having paid attention, not having stretched a little when I was there, when I could risk so much and have so little to lose. As you get more mature, the consequences become a little greater all the time. I think that's probably something I wish I had discovered when I was young.

Q: *How does the spiritual dimension fit in your overall life philosophy?*

A: I'm not a particularly religious person. I have a strong sense that there is a greater being. I guess that's why it's important to me to the extent that I can make a contribution, to touch somebody if you will, to leave a mark on somebody's life or help them through a troubled time. I feel it's a spirituality, I guess, it's a sense of duty and a sense of commitment to humankind. Some folks call it being a good Christian. It doesn't really matter what you call it. It's a matter of being willing to extend yourself beyond your own realm. That's part of the reflection and contemplation, too. It's keeping yourself in perspective.

I may have mentioned this, but we used to live in Idaho a long time ago. I guess we were there about four and a half years. The thing that I found about that topography that was so moving was spending time in the mountains. It was humbling to be such a small thing compared to the scope and magnitude of the mountains. It's hard to put your finger on what chord it strikes in you. The majesty of it and the very size of the mountains — you're just a little pebble.

Conversation with Hal, Chief Executive in a Fortune 500 Company

Hal is 46 years old and has been married for 24 years. Hal's wife, Stacy, is a successful career woman. He has one daughter, and she is in college.

Q: *If you were to define an ideal balanced life for you, how would you define it?*

A: In my everyday life, what I would define as a balanced life ... I don't know if it is obvious or not, but I think that most of us have to work, and the biggest percentage of us — although I think only 50 percent stay together — are married. I see the balance right now in my life as a balance between, obviously, my work and my family. I don't work for myself. I really work for my family, so it wouldn't mean a lot to me just to be working for myself. I'd like to make it more of a balanced life. Plus, a balance within my community, not just work and family. I think it's important that we give back to our community some of the things we might take from it.

I call it stewardship. I look that way in the money that we make in our lifetime. It's really not ours. We are just kind of borrowing it for that period of time and what we do with it is — we like to give it back to our community. To me, that helps keep things balanced. I see balance in life as more of a balance between family, community and business and involving myself in a lot of areas but not trying to overextend myself in any one of them because if I do, I'm probably coming up short in some other areas. To me that's kind of what I'm looking at.

Q: *Looking back, can you recall a time or times when things did get out of balance, and what caused it?*

A: I think that has to do with our maturity and growth — the life cycle, you might say. But I think early on in my life, I felt like I spent more time with my business than I did with my family. I guess it's because I felt like that was what you were supposed to do. When you first start out in the business world, I guess, you're most impressed by the people you are working with, your boss or your leader or whatever. If they're totally devoted to work and working all the time, you have a tendency to lean that way. In fact, that's what everybody does. I found that happened, particularly when I lived in California. I guess, as you start moving away — just like you mentioned earlier, you said "something's a little out of balance here," it just triggers in our mind or in our heart or whatever, but it tells us "I'm veering off here, and I need to get back on course and get a little more participation with my family." I think you do that.

I'm 46 and I am now working with a lot of guys who are 35 to 38, and they are just workaholics. I'm saying to them, "Don't forget, you've got that 12-year-old who is growing up, and she'll be out of your lap before you know it, and you need to spend some time with her too." They will travel like crazy, and they'll work day and night and weekends. I'm already beyond that phase, and I know I went through it. Try to get a little more time with the family. It's not all work, because sometimes you may not have a job, but you still have your family. I saw myself going through the same cycle, and I reflect back on that. I don't know if it is doing any good but that's what I'm doing.

I think that obviously we have external influences, but really what happens, if you're happy with where you are and who you are in your everyday life and your family, then obviously you want to spend more time there. But if you are not, what's the next best thing? Spend a lot of time at work. It's kind of like isolating yourself from other problems or other areas where you're not happy. You do things because you want to be where you are happy. You want to be where you're comfortable. You want to be where you enjoy being.

Some people at certain times of their life, they really enjoy being at work more than they enjoy being at home. I think that happens to us. I think that's kind of human nature to a certain extent. Or people go through that phase, but sometimes it has to come back to them and say, "Wait a minute. What's really a long time?" It's like electricity taking the path of least resistance. People do the same thing — where they are happiest, where they are comfortable. You go through those phases in life and then you say, "Wait a minute, all I've really got is my family or my church." To me it's not just your church and your family and your work. It's your community; it's the whole cycle there that we go through in life. I like the mix, personally. Try to mix it up and take it all in.

Try to get a little more time with the family. It's not all work, because sometimes you may not have a job, but you still have your family.

Q: *Do the people in your life let you know when your life is out of balance?*

A: Well, I can tell you that if I am not in synch with them, they let me know. Then I have to determine in my own mind if they are right or not, and if I agree with them. But if I am spending too much time at work or something, or they think I'm spending too much time at work — right now I'm spending a lot of time traveling, and they let me know that they think I'm spending too much time traveling. So I try to figure out ways to include them. I take my wife and my daughter with me. So that's the only way I know to deal with that. If business is going to require that I travel, then come on and go with me. Let's go together.

I do get input from my external sources that, to me, make a difference. Obviously, I guess, in business, now that I have a boss in New York, if he thinks I'm not spending enough time up there, then he tells me too. We all have those outside influences that pull us either into balance or out of balance. I don't know. I guess it's all how we perceive it. Some people may think that three-quarters work and one-quarter time at home and community is balance. I personally don't.

It changes as we grow. Before, in our early years of work and earning the dollars, we had to be there when the opportunity was there. We had to prove ourselves a lot more, but as we grew in the business and grew into management, you realized that if you work smart, you can have some time away or you can elect to just bury yourself in your job. I'm not financially in the position to where I can say I'm not going to work and just spend all my time with my family. I probably wouldn't be happy doing that anyway.

Q: *Do you feel that to keep experiencing the fulfillment in career, we need to be continually challenged?*

A: You're getting ready to take on a new area that is going to be challenging, but may take a lot more of your time. But we need a challenge. I just took on a new area. I've never done this. I'm doing marketing now. I've always been in sales or operations and running the company. Now I'm getting ready to do marketing for the whole company. To me, it's new and different and it's something I can learn and it's challenging to see if I can pull it off in the next year to year and a half. It's not something that I'm just delighted to do, but I feel like it needs to be done within our company. It is going to take time away from my family, but I have explained to them how I hope we can work it out so that I can go up to New York and they can go with me and get a cottage on the lake and stay on the lake. I think that is kind of getting a balance, reaching a compromise.

Q: *How would you describe the "success" yardstick against which you measure yourself?*

A: I don't think you can measure it in just monetary ways. I think you have to measure it in your own self-growth. I think that's probably where I feel more successful than anything. Just getting to know myself better. By doing that, I can be successful in a lot of other areas, whether it's work or with my family or any other area. Once you get comfortable with yourself and know yourself, then you can be comfortable in most any situation. That to me comes with maturity and growth and stimulation. I felt that that's probably one of the most successful things in my life that I think I've had a pretty good idea about myself. Therefore I can enjoy the rest of my activities in life whether it's family, business, community or whatever. So I think the one thing that I feel a lot more successful about is knowing my capabilities — what I'm capable of doing, what I'm not capable of doing, what I'm secure with and what I'm not secure with. When I'm acting in an insecure way, why I'm frustrated, why I'm not frustrated — to just know that about myself.

One of the things I liked so much about that course (Executive Development Course, based on philosophy, religion, history and humanities at Rhodes College in Memphis) was that it really opened up a lot of ideas and stimulated my mind a lot more. Before, I hadn't done that. I'm not an intellectual person, but it really did generate a lot of thought. I mean I beat the odds if I stay together with my family. I think that's a challenge to work every day to make a marriage work. It doesn't just happen. You've got to work at it. You've got to compromise. You've got to realize when you're right and when you're wrong.

Q: *I've talked to a lot of people, and what you have described is not the norm. This definition that you've come up with, if you were to have been asked 15 years ago, would you have defined it the same way?*

A: No. I'm sure I wouldn't have. My goals were different then. I probably would have defined it more along the lines of ... success to me would be that at age 35 I would be making so much money, at age 40 I would be making so much money, etc. Of course, the house and everything that goes along with it, the material things. I drive a nice car, and I live in a nice house, and I like those things. It's very comfortable to me and I'm very thankful. I'm grateful

> *I think that's a challenge to work every day to make a marriage work. It doesn't just happen. You've got to work at it.*

that I've been able to accomplish that. You know, a lot of that is timing — being in the right place at the right time, making a business decision, growing a business and sharing in the success of the business. Maybe it has to do with the fact that I feel financially comfortable. Prior to the feeling financially comfortable, my definition of success may have been different. I wanted to get to the point where I was financially comfortable. Now, that we basically sold the company last year, or sold our stock, even though I'm in the business, I feel very comfortable so I focus on other things. That may be part of it.

Q: *I was talking to a group of executives downtown, and I went around the room and told them what we were after. These were all successful people like yourself, and most of them put the financial security as priority number-one.*

A: They wanted more financial security, even though they had it?

Q: *Yes. They had it. Again, you never really have enough because there is always some more. The question I posed to them was that we in America are in the top 5 percent of the world in standard of living. People like yourself who are successful business executives are in the top 1 percent of the U.S. population. If you don't feel secure, then the other part of the population should be very unhappy.*

A: I have gone through a lot of that in the last few years because, I guess, as a rule, growing up I didn't focus on that a lot. My wife has been a psychiatric social worker for years, and she has a lot of insight and a good psychological and philosophical background. She has made me focus a little more on that, where most people wouldn't. I am a firm believer that a man is probably as good as the woman behind him or with him. If you don't have somebody that's really there and cares and encourages you to go on and do some of the things. As a rule, I think that women really play an important part in our success in our lives.

Q: *That is, if you allow them.*

A: Yes. There are plenty of people who have wives that could contribute a lot, but they won't let them.

Q: *I have to congratulate you. Not many 46-year-olds have gotten into this much self knowledge. I detect a strong sense of spiritual dimension in you.*

A: Well, that means a lot to me coming from you. I know you think about these things. I appreciate that. I don't know that I am any more mature than most 46-year-olds, but I've been thinking a lot about this sort of thing over that last few years and where I really want to be in five years or two years. I guess some of that helps. I think you think about "Where am I right now, and what's it really all about?" We have gotten quite involved in our church and done the stewardship campaign several times and enjoyed it, and I think I've learned a lot doing it. Maybe it has to do with my mature wife. She rubs off on me.

You know, you really can get caught up in all of that. I don't know why I happen to be in this phase, trying to figure out who I am. I guess some of that just comes from reflecting and thinking about what is going on with life as a whole. I guess we all learn from our experiences. We learn a lot from our experiences, and if we don't, then we've really missed something in life. That happens to a lot of people. A lot of people can go through life, and there is a problem, and they can't see it. A big part of learning is spotting the problem in the first place and then figuring out what to do about it. If you've seen people that work for you and they weren't capable of seeing a problem that exists in the work area, so they certainly couldn't solve it if they didn't even know it was there. Some reason or another, I think I have some intuitiveness about me that can see some problems and spot some problem areas and figure out how to solve them. The same holds true in life itself. Own up to those problems and figure out how to do something about it. That sometimes is not an easy pill to swallow.

Conversation with Susan, University Dean

Susan is married to an attorney, and they have grown children.

Q: *Based on your life experience, how would you define for your-self an ideally balanced life?*

A: For myself, ideally, it's pretty simple. It has to do with doing something that is helping me recognize my potential, as far as I think that I can achieve with my intellect and with my drive for doing something productive. It has to do with having a loving and good relationship with my family and friends. It has to do with having a congenial relationship with a wider group of people, and then it has to do with having a sense of adventure and fun in life, in seeing new places, experiencing new things, and appreciating other people's creativity. Part of that is my own physical well-being, having my body functioning in a way to enjoy all of this, and being not just free from pain, but really feeling, for my age, as capable of physical exertion as possible.

Then there is one other dimension that I think ties it all together, and it's probably what gives it that balance. And that is an awareness and a connection with something that is beyond me and is transcendent. At times in my life, I've called it God. At other times in my life, I call it just the truth or inner sense. It is God, but it is not static. When I was young, God was a paternalistic caring father, and now God is the undefinable manifestation of love, not anthropomorphic but just a reality, a truth of something beyond that connects us all and connects all of reality. When I can attune myself to that, and feel in balance with that force, that is when I feel most in balance with everything else that I mentioned.

Q: *Keeping in mind the balance that you talked about, can you recall a time when your life was out of balance?*

A: Yes. There have been several. See, I've lived a long time.

Q: *Looking at one or two times, what would you say caused your life to get out of balance?*

A: I think one was an internal growth, and one was an external factor that kind of toppled my idea of the way things should be. You probably would like specifics. The internal was that I had grown up in a fairly traditional family, and I had a very happy childhood and had done well in school. And I always knew that I would, at some point, get married, have a family and live happily ever after. That was the dream of my generation. And that's about what I did. I had a lot of good experiences before I met the man I was to marry, but when I met him and when we were married, we had a very traditional relationship. I had a good education up to that point, but I had not planned to use it in any career fashion outside the home, although I had what would be equivalent to a master's degree. After my B.A., I went to the International Graduate School of the University of Stockholm and graduated from there. I've had a fair amount of education for someone of my generation and gender, but still I was totally content and happy with my decision. It was not until my children were all in school and I was approaching 40 that I thought, "My God, is this all there is?" It really started gnawing at me.

Now I realize that I was just going through normal adult

growth and change, and that people don't stop growing and changing at age 21. But I didn't know that at that time, and it was pretty unbalancing and pretty threatening. It made my life miserable. It also made my husband's life miserable. I'm sure that it wasn't too good for the children, but I maintained the structure even though there was a lot of internal turmoil. I needed to change. So, I first started by going back to school, and then I got a job. Through a period of five or six years, there was a tremendous amount of personal adjustment. My husband also had to do a lot of adjusting. Being a lawyer, he saw it as "renegotiating the contract." It got to the point where I had to face some very strong realities — would I rather be married or not married? I came to the conclusion that I'd rather be married, and then I had to say, "Well, who would I like to be married to?" And there wasn't anyone I'd rather be married to than him. So we worked our way out of it — and I do have to say "we."

Although the pressure came from my internal time clock, there were also generational issues in that women younger than I were doing a lot more in the larger world. Mine was in a way the last generation of the traditional approach in the U.S. So that was one time that I was very much out of balance. It was a painful period, but a growth period. I think many times growth requires pain.

It's interesting now, because I see others at that age going through this growth and pain, and I understand, but there is so little I can say to them. I kind of want to hold their hand, but know you can't hold it too much because you know what they're going through is a very personal and individual matter. I feel very fortunate that my growth didn't explode and it didn't dissolve the marriage. It could have so easily. I just feel very lucky. My balance then was re-created on a new level and a new understanding, and I have to attribute it very much to the man I married. It takes two to achieve that kind of understanding. When it was obvious that I wanted to work and develop my talents outside the home, it took tremendous growth and adjustment, a transformation of our selves and our relationship.

Another factor that just really exploded my world — well, there were several things, come to think of it. But one I guess I want to mention was when I realized my father had Alzheimer's. That was very, very difficult for me to accept because I had a fairly simplistic faith and believed that a person's soul was the spark of life. For him to be alive, yet seemingly having no life or no rational being, was very, very disturbing to me. I couldn't deal with that conceptually. What had happened to him? What had happened to his soul? I had to come to terms with his body being there in this lifeless state. Now looking back on it, I was forced to a redefining of my whole approach to ... spiritual reality. I started to say "religion," but I don't want to use the term "religion." Religion to me is the structure under which people come to terms with spiritual reality. I think there are many wonderful traditions. I am still part of a tradition, but I know that my beliefs, at this point, are not doctrinaire at all. They are just what I came to through that experience in developing a new understanding.

I totally lost my faith for a while because we had been very close. My father was my ideal. He had been my mentor and had been such a wonderful person to me. I just couldn't spiritually deal with this condition or my grief. It was almost a relief when he finally died, but there was a period of seven years. There was some guilt, too, because he was on the West Coast and I was here in Memphis, and we were so distant I couldn't be with him. In response to your question, there was a lot going on there that threw me off balance.

As my children became adults with their own problems, my balance was again threatened. I realized I am someone who wants to fix things, and there were some things in their lives that I had no control to fix. I was beginning to learn acceptance of situations and realities I could not change. This was a new approach for me. I think that there was a point in my life where I thought you achieved balance if you could control all of the factors in your life and when you put them together, you had a neat little package. In a number of areas this was not working. I had to come to terms with the fact that the way you really have balance is when you let loose and you just know that you are living in the moment. That's all you can really manage. You have a lot of faith that there are some bigger truths, and they are going to take care of things and the people you love. You have to accept you can't affect someone else's behavior. You are only responsible for your own. This was a new way of viewing my role as a mother.

I just realized that in response to your question on balance I've been talking about my role as a wife, my role as daughter and my role as a mother. I've been talking about a female, a woman, trying to come to terms with what her balance is in those roles as she seeks her own individuality in life and career.

Q: *On an ongoing basis, what ideas or activities do you use to help you maintain your life balance?*

A: On an ongoing basis, they are pretty prosaic. I know that I maintain better balance if I eat right and get good exercise. Sometimes that's just forcing myself to do good, particularly the exercise part of it. I have a lot of nervous energy, and I just feel and think better and don't get quite as introspective if I exercise regularly. I also have carved out a little time each day where I am just quiet. I have tried to learn meditation and have had some success. I do at least recognize that if I can stop my mind from racing, some creative insights and peace of mind come, and at work I try very much to be present when I'm with people. I am also a proverbial list maker, and I try to just keep the length reasonable. I really do know what I can accomplish, and what I can't accomplish. I have to give up. That's what I try to do. And another thing, which is not so much something to do, but an attitude. I've learned not to be as hard and judgmental on myself. I am not perfect, but if I do the best I can, that's the best I can do. Sometimes I probably don't even do the best I can, but I do what I can do in a situation. Realizing this helps me to maintain my balance.

Q: *Now, that must have taken some time to arrive at that.*

A: Yes. Well, remember, I'm 58 years old.

Q: *For driven people like myself, it's very hard to say, "Well, I did my best." Instead the reaction is "Why did I make that mistake?"*

A: Sure, and you do think it, but you can try to gain some perspective. I don't beat up on myself the way I used to. I don't feel the guilt and the self-deprecation. Part of it, and this was the hardest thing I had to learn in life, was to learn to become self-assured rather than find my approval from others. I think most of my life I was looking for that assuredness and that feedback and that approval from others. I'm still not there. We are always learning. We were talking earlier about those little hooks where you find yourself falling back into a habit or attitude trap. It's kind of your tape, your old tape of the way you used to think and feel. And when I find myself too concerned about what other people are thinking, I see that as a trap back into self-defeating behavior. I recognize that I may not be right, but I try to operate from a base of open self-assuredness, knowing that's the only way I'm going to be able to function without this guilt and this self-deprecation. I never can be perfect in mine or someone else's eyes, because no one is capable of perfection.

I probably perform as well, and I think it also gives me the quality to not take things as personally. For instance, at work when things were not going well, or when I was at cross purposes with someone, I used to have a tendency to get very angry and take it personally. I wouldn't show my anger, because I am too much of a lady, but I would internalize it or blame myself and be very frustrated because I couldn't make the other person understand. Now I can say, "Look, that's his agenda." And that's OK. I may disagree and I can be much more open about it. I'll do everything I can to change that agenda, but if I can't, that's the way it is. I may feel like I am not accomplishing as much, because I am used to so much internal pressure that no longer builds. It is as if I have more time since so much of my time used to be spent worrying, or on unproductive thoughts. I expect a lot from others around me and work hard to make sure my expectations of them and theirs of me are understood. I try to never demand more of anyone else than I demand of myself. There is a real art in establishing a balanced work team. It takes constant attention.

Q: *Let me ask you — in your position and with the demands on your time, you had mentioned that the ideal balance was to find time for doing your leisure things and some time for yourself and the family. How do you handle these demands on your personal time from work and social obligations?*

A: I have changed my life a lot. I have given up many of the social aspects of my life. I realize that because of my job, I have a lot of social obligations with receptions and meetings and such as that. Before I had this job, I was a much more social person just out in the community, and had a lot more parties and activities with friends. I did a lot more entertaining privately in the home than I do now because I don't enjoy it as much, or I don't have the time to do it. Now, that's still a little problem as far as my husband goes. I think he would enjoy doing more entertaining. That's a compromise, but I can't do that and do a good job here, and do the other things that are necessary, such as my own private quiet time, and sports time and just pure leisure time where I am not responsible for social exchange. I need sometimes to just play.

So, I recognize there are some things I have to give up. I used to play a lot more tennis, and that's where I got my exercise. I now run or swim, which is solitary, but it can be done on my own time. It's not skill building and it's not as much fun, but it makes the total life balance easier. One goes through phases or segments of life. There was a period when I was playing tennis every day. There was another time when I was doing a lot of social activities. I feel very, very lucky because I have had these choices. Now, since I have the responsibility of my job, and I feel that there is so much that can be done here, I focus most of my energies on this job. That means that my other energies I have for my family, my few close friends — which I don't really see much — it's really more my family and

> *Responsibility is something you choose. You choose the responsibilities that you have, and then how you handle them I think is part of that balancing act.*

my job right at this time in my life. I might work 12 or 14 hours a day for a week, and then I don't feel any guilt in just taking a short trip and playing. It's not a balance every day, but being aware of your whole life and your choices. I think responsibility is something you choose. You choose the responsibilities that you have, and then how you handle them I think is part of that balancing act.

Q: *How would you describe the success yardstick against which you measure yourself?*

A: I think I've made choices, and I think if I had made different choices, I might have been more successful. Like when we were talking about writing this book — this is something we talked about before. I still don't know if I'm kidding myself that there is a book within me, but I obviously am not making the choice to write it. So there, I'm unsuccessful. I have a goal that I do not accomplish. As far as in this job, by very modest standards I've been successful. I've taken a division that was non-existent and built up a pretty good program, but by other standards, it's kind of puny. I see so much that could be accomplished and I get frustrated — not frustrated — yeah, I guess frustrated. I continually think about what should be done. I know there is more, so I am always looking. I don't know if I'm answering you.

Q: *I was trying to look at your success. Would that be success in the job or "Susan is a successful person"?*

A: I think success is a very relative term, and I think it also varies with where you are in life, in your age. Success is a word, and I know I'm not typical. That doesn't mean a great deal to me. Success generally is not something I strive for. I strive for particulars. I strive for a good marriage. At this stage, who knows what will happen tomorrow? At this point, I have a very good marriage. So yes, I am successful. I have a wonderful relationship, or I feel like I have a good relationship with all of my children. I have a close relationship with two of them. I feel very fortunate. So much of what gives me happiness I feel is not my doing. Even the job that I have — if I look at it objectively, yes, I have been successful. But what I take satisfaction in I would not strictly call "success." Living up to my potential would probably be a criteria upon which I would judge satisfaction. Have I accomplished this? I probably have in some areas and probably not in others. It is a moving target.

Q: *What process do you use when your life balance and your husband's life balance come into conflict?*

A: That, here again, has changed over time. The process we go through when there is conflict is to try to get the real issue out on the table at the beginning. So many times when people are in conflict, it's not about what they say it's about. Sometimes it is very difficult to find the source of the conflict. That is easily said, but very difficult to achieve. I think the willingness on both of our parts to seek a resolution, realizing there was never a time when it was going to be all my way or all his way, has been essential. I think there was always a recognition and a basic respect for the other. We believed there had to be a way to reach an understanding. We both knew resolution could be achieved if we just understood what the problem was. If it got too emotional or the conflict was too great, sometimes a time out, just cooling off, was necessary.

This comes through a lot of growth together and going through hard times together. We learned that each of our needs are different at different times, and being respectful of those needs, and knowing that we cannot fulfill each other's needs completely helped. He has to have a balance that goes beyond me, and I too, have needs apart from him. That was part of what we had to come to terms with. We don't answer each other's every need. In fact, at this point, I'm not sure we even think of it in terms of needs any more. I think when you are younger you are more dependent, but now it's more of a very basic mutual respect and friendship and love. The process for resolving the conflict has been varied and difficult at times.

Q: *And there was a compromise on your part?*

A: Sure, and cooling-off periods.

Q: *The reason I was asking this questions was because the demands on both of your time are great, and that must impact the time together.*

A: That's a good point. We really enjoy traveling together. We now do quite a bit of sailing. That's something that doesn't affect his job or mine. We find some things that we just enjoy, just being together and doing things together. That has been a very, very important factor in our relationship.

Q: *Just to get away?*

A: Yes. And there was a time I think he was jealous of the time I spent in my job, and there was a time when I was jealous of the time he spent that did not include me. Now I don't worry about that. I don't concern myself with that. He really has gotten so he doesn't concern himself if I am convinced it is something I should do. But keeping him informed is so important so he can make his own plans. It used to be that I would feel guilty about having to do this or that, or asking him to do something I knew he did not want to do. Now he asks, "Do you want me to do this with you?" Unless I really want him to be there, I just say "no." And it's OK. I used to be equivocal and not want to commit. I think the clearer I am in what I want and what I need, and at the same time try to be fair and respect his needs, the better we get along. So many times I think people's perception of what they should do is so different from what they really want done.

Q: *As you say, it's a growth process. They haven't taken time to* *say, "Hey, it's OK for me to be doing things if he's not there or she's not there."*

A: Sure. In the last analysis I am not judged by his behavior or what he does. That was a very hard thing for me to realize. We are two separate people who choose to be together. I'm my own person, and what I contribute and get from our relationship is that mutuality. He gives me tremendous support, and I think I do the same for him.

Conversation with Cathy, Registered Nurse

Cathy works at a children's hospital. Her husband is a realestate executive. They have three boys, ages 11 years, 7 years, and 9 months.

Q: *Based on your life experiences, how would you define for yourself an ideal balanced life?*

A: OK. I do like to work, so it would definitely include something outside the home, generally on a part-time basis and time with my family, friends, husband, and some time just for myself, too. Is that specific enough?

Q: *Yes. Why is the time for yourself important?*

A: There are things that I do like to do when nobody else is around, and that always seems to be the part that I have the hardest time finding. Just reading a book — by the time I pick up a book at night, usually I'm ready to fall asleep. Just little things like that. Getting exercise on a regular basis. More creative things that sometimes I let go because there are other things that have to be done.

Q: *Keeping in mind that this is what you like to do, can you recall a time in your life when you couldn't find time to do all of these things and did not enjoy the kind of balance you described?*

A: Oh, yes. All the time. I'm still working toward that goal. The hardest times probably were after each of the kids were born — trying to get back to work, having a baby at home. That's always a major adjustment. I guess that's probably an adjustment for anybody. At the time, I think I was trying to do more than I should do, and it got pretty hairy. There were times when I thought, "I just can't do all of this." Then I'd find a way of making it better, cutting back on work or getting help for myself.

Q: *You mentioned after the birth of the children. Any other reason or environment or change?*

A: Probably with the move, when we would relocate. That just tends to be kind of a stressful time, adjusting to a new environment, not knowing your way around, not having friends or family to support you maybe when you could use somebody to help you, feeling like you're all alone. I'm trying to think if there were any other times. I guess there was a period of time when I was in a job that I really didn't like. That was a hectic schedule. I didn't have a real good schedule, and that didn't work out very well. I can't really think of any other times that were really difficult.

Q: *You work part-time?*

A: Yes, it's part-time full-time — two 12-hour shifts. By the hospital, it's considered a full-time position, but it really is only 24 hours of the week.

Q: *Why did you choose the weekend?*

A: Well, for a number of different reasons. One, it was a good package deal as far as what the hospital offers. If you work those shifts, they pay you better, and you have all your benefits. Two, my husband is home then to help out with the children. It solved all my childcare problems. Three, it was a nice set schedule. I can go in, and for 48 hours I do nothing but work and sleep, basically. But then Monday through Friday, I have all my time.

Q: *With three small children and the career on the weekend, do you still feel at times that you can't find time to do all the things you want to do?*

A: Definitely. I think people probably look at it like I've got Monday through Friday with nothing to do, but that's not really the case, as any mother would know. First of all, Monday I sleep, so it takes me until Tuesday to more or less get back in the groove, and then I'm still sometimes tired. And by that time, the laundry is all piled up from the weekend, and the house needs to be cleaned, so that's another couple of days. Then shopping and the kids' school work and the kids' science projects and meetings at school. It's a very full life, and it's a constant challenge.

Q: *So you feel that pretty much you have control over the week, or still some things happen that disturb the weekly routine?*

A: I think overall I have pretty good control. It seems you never do know what's going to happen from one week to the next though. Sometimes all it takes is one of the children getting sick or maybe company from out of town — just extra things that just happen. I feel sometimes I lose control of where I'd like to keep things, but usually if I just allow myself enough time and try to relax about things and not be an ultra-perfectionist, things work out.

Q: *How would you describe the "success" yardstick against which you measure yourself?*

A: That is so funny, because Anthony, my husband, was just saying, "Maybe the reason he wants to interview you is because we're a successful family." I don't really think that much about being successful, but I guess maybe we are. We have three children that we think are just wonderful, and

> *Sometimes I lose control of where I'd like to keep things, but usually if I just allow myself enough time and try to relax about things and not be an ultra-perfectionist, things work out.*

everything is going well in their lives, which we're happy about so far. They're still young, but so far they're doing well. We've got a solid marriage. It's a first time marriage for both of us. We feel very intact, which so many people don't have now. My husband has a good job. I've got a good job. I've got a life outside of the house, which is nice. I don't know. I think you just have to find happiness within yourself, just kind of get to that point where you say, "Yes, I'm happy." I guess that's success.

Q: *How long have you been married?*

A: Thirteen and a half years.

Q: *With three small children and all the activities, do you find that sometimes it is hard to make time for each other?*

A: Yes. Once again, especially because of my schedule. More people have their weekends together, and instead of being together on the weekends it may be husband and wife going out on Saturday night. I'm going to work, and he is staying home with the children. We don't have a lot of time just with each other, but we do have a lot of family time, which is what we both enjoy. Once or twice a month, we do try to go out just together or socially with another couple or whatever. I think we're both satisfied with the amount of time that we have together. I think we meet each other's needs in that way.

Q: *Are there times you feel stress from work or whatever kind of carries over into the home life, or home life into work, or you sometimes have things on your mind?*

A: Yes. Sometimes — well, I guess it does go both ways. Sometimes I might go to work and just be in a bad mood from whatever. Something at home hasn't been good, or it's been a horrible week or a horrible day, or I'm upset with my husband or my children or whatever, and I'll get to work and be unhappy, just be a grouch. Usually what I find is that being away from the home and in a different situation, before too long I'm focusing on my work and leaving my problems behind. I think it turns out to be a healthy thing, because then sometimes when I go home, I feel better. I've had time away. Maybe the problems go away while I'm at work or whatever. It's kind of just a different focus, I guess, a different perspective. Maybe things aren't as I thought they were. As far as carrying my problems from work home, truthfully, Monday morning when I leave work, I pretty much leave work until Saturday night when I go back. I mean there are a lot of emotional situations, obviously, being a nurse at a children's hospital, there are some real sorry things that we have to deal with. But I'm pretty much able, once I leave, like I said, I leave it behind me. I don't really have a problem with that.

Q: *You are active in the church — so spirituality plays a big role in your life?*

A: I think it does. I think it plays into everything. Just having that support helps you through just about everything.

Q: *I think, as you said, we talked initially that when you define your life balance, these are your priorities. You find time for your children and family and work.*

A: Yes, and for friends. I do have some real good female — mainly — friendships, and that's important.

Q: *Very important. Is there anything different in a woman's environment about the balanced-life issues than in a man's?*

A: Well, I think so, simply because I think women still carry more of the responsibility at home. I think I'm fortunate because my husband plays a real strong role helping raise the children. I think we're 50-50 when it comes to the children. I know other families where that's just not the case. The woman makes all the decisions for the children and really runs the whole show at home and doesn't have much help. I'm thinking of one person in particular. I feel sorry for her. But I think that's a key difference between men and women. I think men are more able to just come home from work and sit in the chair — but I might be wrong there. There's probably a whole other side to this story too, but I still think that old traditional role of the man able to come home and have his dinner and sit in the chair, I think that still probably exists. Maybe not as much as it did but I think women probably have more different things to balance. That's why I certainly would not want to be in the shoes of any woman who has to work 40 hours a week, Monday through Friday, and then come home to a family and all of that. I don't know how they do it. I honestly don't know how a woman does all of that.

Q: *You will entertain the possibility of working full-time when your kids are grown?*

A: Possibly, I don't know. I don't know if career is ever going to be that important to me. I foresee working because, like I said, I do enjoy working, but as far as really aspiring to a much higher level career, I don't know that I ever will, and I don't know that I will work 40 hours a week.

Q: *Did you work full-time before the kids were born?*

A: Well, it didn't really work out that way. I finished school and had a baby, just about like that. And then I started working. I had my children a little bit sooner than I thought I was going to. I did work full-time for a while after I had Chad, for a few years. It was OK, but it got stressful. With two children, I just couldn't do it. I really just can't understand how a woman can keep up with full-time work and everything at home.

Interview with Carolyn, Author and Law Professor

Carolyn is a law professor who is married and has three young children. Her spouse is also a university professor. The interview with Carolyn focuses on particular concerns that women experience in attaining balanced life.

Q: *Based on your life experiences, how would you define for yourself a balanced life?*

A: I don't know that I could say I have achieved it, but I think that feeling less conflicted and being able to focus more exclusively on one major interest at a time would help me to feel more in balance. I know that my priorities are my family and my work, and that when they are in competition with one another I feel out of balance.

This past Christmas was a wonderful time of feeling the peace and contentment that comes with balance. I finished giving exams and then put my work completely aside during the Holidays and focused my attention on the family. We sang songs, baked cookies, decorated the house and generally enjoyed the holiday season. I felt really connected with my family. When it was time to go back to work, I was ready to give it my full attention and energy.

It's necessary for me to compartmentalize my life to an extent so that I can give adequate attention to whatever I am doing. Whenever I am trying to do several things at once they come into conflict, and I don't enjoy any of them very much. Quality time at work and at home are both very important — I couldn't do without either. When my first child was born I enjoyed him so much that I entertained the idea of taking some leave time from work to be at home full-time for a while. We now have three children, and I realize that I need work as much as I need family, and that I probably would not be completely happy without my work.

On the other hand, I look at my friends who have chosen not to have children or who have full-time, live-in sitters who provide most of the daily care for their children, and I realize that I wouldn't be happy with that either. I want to spend time with my children on a regular basis, and I couldn't do that if I made a commitment to a job that required extensive travel or regular 18-hour days. My current choice allows me to be flexible in my scheduling so that I can have afternoons at home with the children after school. I do come up a little short on sleep sometimes, as I usually do several hours of work each evening after they have gone to bed. This past week, I put aside a project one evening to watch my sons' first gymnastics lesson. The work was there waiting when I got home, but I wouldn't have missed seeing the expressions on their faces for anything. It was worth the lost sleep.

> *This past week, I put aside a project one evening to watch my sons' first gymnastics lesson. The work was there waiting when I got home, but I wouldn't have missed seeing the expressions on their faces for anything. It was worth the lost sleep.*

Q: *On an ongoing basis, what ideas and activities continue to help you maintain your life balance?*

A: One thing that makes a big difference in my life is my spouse's commitment to sharing the parenting of our children. I know a lot of husbands who "help" their wives with the children, but I don't know many who share the commitment and responsibility to the extent that we do. I probably worry about it more, but there's a real commitment there on both our parts to balance our personal and professional commitments.

We have both given up a lot of personal time in order to give a significant quality and quantity of time to our careers and to our children.

Q: *How do you compensate for that?*

A: I compensate by branching out in creative ways at work.

Taking on a new or creative project that's related to my work often allows me contact with interesting people and a creative outlet that meets some of my personal needs beyond career and family.

Q: *Do you agree that unresolved personal/off-the-job concerns adversely affect performance on-the-job and vice versa?*

A: I call it "memory overload." Sometimes I am juggling so many different responsibilities and activities that it is hard to give full attention to anyone. If I get overloaded at work, that comes home. And if I'm overloaded at home, that comes to work with me.

Q: *How would you describe the "success" yardstick against which you measure yourself?*

A: That's a hard one. Sometimes I will be listening to someone say to me, "I just don't know how you do it all!" And all the while, I'm thinking the same thing about her! Sometimes I really don't know how any of us does it.

Women of our generation don't have many role models or road maps to follow. For many of us, our mothers were full-time homemakers, and it is easy to compare our own parenting and homemaking to that of women who were able to devote full-time to that task alone. I remember my mother managed our home and five children, and I thought she was pretty busy. I now realize she had time to play bridge during the day. I wouldn't even think of playing bridge during the day — or any other time. I don't have that kind of personal time.

It doesn't work very well to measure myself against colleagues who do not also have family responsibilities. They are able to devote more time and energy to their careers than I am at this point.

The best way I can measure my own success is in personal and job satisfaction. When I compare myself to other people whose choices and lifestyles differ from my own, I realize I wouldn't trade places with any of them. As long as I am happy

with my own life, then that is the most effective measure of
my success.

Conversation with Beverly, Graphic Designer

Beverly is a freelance graphic designer. She is a divorced mother of a 7-year-old daughter.

Q: *How would you define for yourself the ideal balance in your
life?*

A: I guess balance to me is everything working in concert
together and being able to meet the needs of all the different
aspects of your life — children and work and home.

Q: *Being a single mother puts many extra demands on you. How
do you manage to maintain the balance?*

A: Well, I'm not sure I always maintain it. I'm fairly recently a
single mother. I just got divorced six months ago, though I was
separated for about 10 months before that. The hardest thing
has been having to do everything that needs to be done, literally. You get dependent on having somebody else there who
can keep your child while you run to the grocery store, or who
is working in the yard while you are doing something in the
house, that kind of thing. Suddenly you have all the responsibilities, and it's hard.

I think the way you deal with that is you have to stop and
set priorities. You have to look at all the different aspects of
your life and think about what is important to you and what
deserves your time and what you want to put your time into.
Then you make decisions based on that.

Very early on in my single motherhood, I decided that my
child was the priority for me and that I would do whatever was
needed to meet her needs first. Then everything else kind of
follows in place behind that. That means sometimes the house
isn't as spic and span as I might like for it to be. It means that

although I have to do all the yard work, it's not a high priority for me. I get around to doing it when I can.

But at the same time you don't want to totally let your child's needs take over your life. I have to think about myself too, because there are certain things that I need and certain things that satisfy me that I need to do because that makes me a better mom for her. That's where the balancing act comes in. Trying to keep all of that working together is the tricky part. It's just on a day-to-day basis. I think a mother is always weighing all of the things that need to be done and deciding what she's going to do now and what can wait.

Q: *Being in your own business as you are, you have demands from clients and deadlines. How do you work around those?*

A: There is constant up and down — you can have too much work and you're stressed out, or you don't have enough work, which equates to less money and that kind of worry. One of the reasons I stay in it is to maintain the flexibility, to be available to pick up my daughter from school in the afternoon and bring her home and do her homework with her, to not have her go to a daycare situation so she can have some "down" time, and to be able to go on field trips with her occasionally, to be able to stay home with her if she's sick. The other side of that is that I have to make very efficient use of the time that I have available, so that's made me work a little better, a little more efficiently. It's definitely tough sometimes.

When I have a whole lot of work to do and not as much time as I would like to give to it, then there are times when I get sort of short tempered and preoccupied because I'm thinking about what I need to be doing out in my studio, while I'm actually in the house doing something with my daughter or fixing supper or doing all of those things. Because my studio is physically separate from the house, after she goes to bed, I won't go back out there — I won't leave her alone in the house at night. So one way I am dealing with that is by getting a second computer for the house. From one point of view I think, why would I want to work at night instead of relaxing and taking it easy?

Well, I do if I can. But there were times I would just get frantic because I had so much work to do and not enough time to do it. I don't intend to go to work as soon as I put her to bed every night because then I think I would burn out pretty quickly, but it gives me a backup. It gives me kind of a safety cushion where if I'm really busy and have a lot to do, I know I'll have access to a means of doing it.

Q: *The decision to be self-employed, was it after you got divorced or were you in this business before?*

A: I've been self-employed for 12 years now. There have been a number of times when I was tempted to go to work for someone else and get a regular paycheck and have regular hours. It is certainly easier to focus on your working life, I think, if you are working somewhere other than at home. It is something of a distraction. But again, there was a conscious decision made when I moved my office home when my daughter was born. At that time, I thought it was a good idea to be physically removed from the house so that there was a clear delineation between home and office. I think it would have been very difficult for a small child to understand that Mom's at work and that you can't go be with her all the time. It worked very well when she was young and when there were two of us here — two parents — so that Dad could stay in the house while Mom went out and caught up on work a little bit.

Q: *Is your daughter pretty aware and respectful of your needs now that Mom is trying to work?*

A: Pretty much, but she is only seven years old. She is still in the mindset where she thinks, "If I need something I need it now. Why can't you stop and get me a snack?" But mostly she is very good about that. There have been situations when I was really against a deadline and she was very understanding, very mature in bringing some books out to the studio to sit and read for awhile while I got some work done. I think it will be better now that I have the in-house computer, so she can be in the house with her toys and her books if I have to catch up on some work.

Q: *So what I've heard is that the tradeoffs you've been making is there's certain time for your daughter and for work. How do you fit in time for yourself?*

A: Well, that's something that has been sort of a positive after-effect of the divorce. My ex-husband has our daughter every other weekend, and I have found that having time to myself is so rejuvenating. I realize now it's something that I needed all along. I've always been pretty much of a loner and needed a lot of solitude to kind of recharge my batteries. I guess I didn't realize how much I needed it. During my marriage, it wasn't offered and I didn't demand it, so it was like a constant drain on me. Now every other weekend, my daughter goes to spend the weekend with her dad, and I get time to myself.

It doesn't mean that every other weekend I get to sit down and read a book. But I know that my time is my own to be structured how I need for it to be, whether I want to work in the yard or if I need to catch up on something in my studio or if I just want to sit and read or go shopping. That to me is very renewing. It's one of those situations where you don't realize how bad you feel until you're beyond it, and then you can look back and think, *this feels a lot better.*

It's kind of a female thing I think to be so selfless, to give

> *It's kind of a female thing, I think, to be so selfless, to give your all, to fulfill this person's needs and that person's needs, and do this and do that, and suddenly you discover you've been drained dry and there are no reserves left. That just adds to the problems.*

your all, to fulfill this person's needs and that person's needs, and do this and do that, and suddenly you discover you've been drained dry and there are no reserves left. That just adds to the problems. Having some time to myself has really been a good thing. I regret that I didn't demand it before, because I think it would have been good for the marriage. I would have had a much better outlook, been a much happier person if I had just had a little time to myself to be able to build up my reserves.

Q: *Is there a social need, friends and such, that comes into the balance?*

A: Yes. Throughout the time before and during the divorce, I've had a lot of support from family and from friends, and have rediscovered some that I had sort of lost touch with along the way. That's something else that some people have a tendency to do — I know I did. You know, you get married and get all wound up in your immediate situation and either don't have time or don't have the inclination to reach beyond that and maintain contact with your friends. So another positive thing that has come out of the divorce has been renewing some friendships and making contact with some people that I had not talked to in a long time. That has been very reassuring, a very positive thing.

Q: *Can you recall times when your life did get out of balance and what you had to do to get back?*

A: I have often through my life — especially as an adult — felt that it was so wonderful that when I was having problems with relationships that I had my work to turn to. My work was very solid, and I enjoyed going to it and could kind of forget about my problems and just work. So in a way, that's a balance — you can retreat to a place where you feel secure and happy and competent. And then there were exactly the opposite times when I was unhappy with work, getting tired of the job, that kind of thing. So then you kind of shift back over to your family, and it's nice that you have them to depend on for their support. That balance has been sort of a recurring theme in my life.

But then there have been times when things were going bad on the personal front and bad on the work front, and you think, *Where do I go now?* And that's when things get out of balance. I think you go through life trying to chart that course and depending on always having something — a kind of a life preserver to hang onto, and maybe sometimes going from one to the other. But I think that I have been fortunate in having usually felt like I was pretty well supported on one front or the other — even through some very difficult times. Being self-employed and being successful at it is very difficult, but it's very confidence-building to be able to succeed for 12 years as I have, and to have good clients who really trust me and depend on me and keep coming back to me. It's a source of a lot of satisfaction and self-esteem to have that.

Q: *How would you describe the success, the yardstick that you measure against — or do you even think about this?*

A: If I had to come up with some sort of a definition — it's being at peace. You know, I don't know how to describe it except that way. You feel like you have everything in that balance and no matter what happens, you can deal with it. You have the tools. You have the support system. Being at peace is one way to describe it, but it's somehow deeper than that.

Q: *Is there a spiritual dimension to that?*

A: Yes, certainly. In the last few years I've gotten more involved with my church, and initially the big attraction to the church was the sense of community, because I really liked the people there and I really felt good when I was around them. But as I have gotten more and more involved in the church, I have really begun to feel that there is a spiritual force, a reason things happen, and I'm very comfortable with that. There are things that seem initially bad, but in the long run when you are able to get through it and look back, you can see why it happened. And that gives me a lot of comfort, a lot of peace.

Q: *Is there any process or activity you use to remind yourself what your priorities are?*

A: Not a conscious process. You know, I think every time I look at my child's face, I am reminded of what a miracle she is and how grateful I am to have her and how much joy she brings me. And having the retrospective on the recent couple of years of knowing that I'm a strong person and I can make it through adversity and come out on the other end of it even stronger and hopefully better, makes me feel good about myself. And the realization that having some time to myself — how good it makes me feel. I frequently tell my daughter, who gets a little bit sad when we have to be separated every other weekend, that it makes us appreciate each other more. It makes me feel better about myself to have a little time alone, which makes me a better mom. And she understands.

Q: *Is there anything else you would like to add?*

A: When I was thinking about talking to you, the thing that kept coming back to me was the aspect that sometimes you get so mired down in your problems and difficulties that the concept of balance ... you just feel like it's out of reach. You really have to stop and reassess and set priorities to make yourself come to terms with where you have to go from here. Otherwise you're just struggling to survive.

Q: *Yes, especially when life is so fast paced you just get caught up, and before you know a year has gone by and you just say, "Whoa, where did the year go?" And there isn't much reinforcement from society. They congratulate you on your new house or new car, but nobody asks if you are happy.*

A: That's right. They focus so much on the concrete symbols of success, and I think that most of society doesn't really realize that there are other measures that are far more important. Big houses, fancy cars — they're all fairly transient. I can even look back on the divorce and think that, in some ways, it was a worthwhile experience to go through, just for having made me stop and think and realize some things that I had been blind to for so long. You just get so caught up in day-to-day living that you don't allow yourself the luxury, you don't realize that you need to stop and think of the bigger picture.

9

Balanced Life Lessons from Nature

A life in harmony with nature, the love and of virtue, will purge the eyes to understand her text. By degrees we may come to know the primitive senses of the permanent objects of nature, so that the world shall be to us an open book, and every form significant of its hidden life and final cause.

— Ralph Waldo Emerson

NATURE PROVIDES US WITH SIX KEY lessons in balanced life:

1. Living things in nature want to grow. If a plant or a tree is not growing, it is dead.
2. To live and grow requires an ecologically balanced environment.
3. When the ecological balance is disturbed, the plants and marine life begin to die.
4. The beauty is that life and growth resume once the ecological balance is restored.
5. Restoration of the ecological balance requires action toward changing the pollution causing behavior.
6. The behavioral change and the restoration of ecological balance take time, but persistent action does make it happen.

Let us take a detailed look at each of the six lessons.

1. Living things in nature want to grow. Just like the plants and trees, growth is a basic human need. For an apple tree, the growth is sprouting a new branch. The branch becomes strong, sprouting a flower and then an apple — all manifestations of growth.

Similarly, a child experiences growth when she or he takes the first steps or learns to say "mama" and "dada." As adults, we experience growth in the Career Self when we learn new skills or solve a challenging problem.

We experience growth in the People Self by making new friends or by making existing relationships deeper. We experience growth in the actualizing self when we grow spiritually. We experience growth in the Leisure Self, for example, when we finally master that overhead shot in tennis.

The growth need is met when a person does something or experiences something that is new to him or her. It does not matter to an apple tree that there are millions of other apple trees that have produced apples. It is growth for the apple tree that it has grown and is producing apples.

Similarly, it is growth for the student that she has solved the chemistry equation. It does not matter that thousands before her solved the same problem. For a sales professional, it is growth that he has closed a sale with a tough client.

Each of the above examples shows growth and creativity in action at a personal level. I've noticed that the achievement-driven individuals deprive themselves of satisfaction by not acknowledging this growth. By focusing solely on coming up with, for example, the creative marketing strategy that no one else has thought of, the marketing professional never measures up to his high standard. Creativity and growth means doing something we have not done before.

2. To live and grow requires an ecologically balanced environment. The plants need a healthy balance of sunlight, water and nutrition from the soil. Too much water and not enough sunlight disturbs the balance and retards the plant growth. Too much sunlight and not enough water does the same thing. The simple act of moving the houseplant closer to a window restores the balance and the growth.

I don't know what the botanical name is of a plant in my den, but I call it a zebra plant because its leaves have stripes like a zebra. When there is not enough moisture in the soil, the leaves become droopy, and I know it is a signal to water the plant.

Similarly, the droopy, tired eyes or dragging body at the end of the day or week is sending signals that the life is out of balance. For us to experience growth and become the beautiful person we're capable of becoming, we have to lead a balanced lifestyle — a lifestyle allowing time for career, people, actualization and leisure in a balanced manner.

3. When the ecological balance is disturbed, the plants and marine life begin to die. We've all read of how once-healthy lakes became polluted and the marine life disappeared. Or how, in some rivers or lakes where the marine life is not completely dead, the growth has been retarded, and the size of the fish is much smaller than before. Lake Erie experienced loss of marine life in its polluted state 20 or so years ago.

> *Our growth as a human being is stifled when our lifestyle becomes unbalanced. The vitality, the inner energy stops renewing itself, and we feel restless and tired.*

Similarly, our growth as a human being is stifled when our lifestyle becomes unbalanced. The vitality, the inner energy stops renewing itself, and we feel restless and tired. We go through the motions and may even have many external trappings of success, but feel unfulfilled as human beings.

4. The beauty is that life and growth resume once the ecological balance is restored. The ecological balance in Lake Erie has been restored and the marine life is thriving again. Similarly, our vitality and inner energy spring back into life as soon as we start leading a balanced lifestyle.

After leading a balanced life just for a week, we can experience a life that is full of richness. Just as the unpolluted air refreshes the body, the balanced life refreshes the inner self. For example, science has also proven that the lungs and the heart begin to resume their efficiency once the pollution in the form of cigarette smoke is eliminated from the body.

We drive hundreds of miles to Yellowstone, Yosemite and other national parks to see nature's beauty in its natural, unpolluted state. Why?

"A nobler want of man is served by nature, namely, the love of beauty," Emerson said. Just as nature is beautiful in its unpolluted state, so is a human being. There is a natural radiance from within on the face of a person enjoying inner harmony.

5. Restoration of the ecological balance requires action toward changing the pollution causing behavior. To clean Lake Erie, an analysis had to be done first as to what was disturbing the ecological balance. Once the pollutants were identified, then action had to be taken to clean up the lake.

Similarly, if a person's life is out of balance, then some action must be taken to bring it back in balance. It won't happen if he or she continues with the same lifestyle.

The Balanced Life Four-Step Process introduced in the first chapter is the key to restoring the balance. Take a moment to review the four steps.

1. Visualizing the balanced, healthy state, and taking charge of your life.

2. Identifying the root causes of imbalance in your life — the internal as well as the external root causes.

3. Developing a personal action plan to address the root causes identified in Step 2.

4. Taking action to implement the plan. Got to do it!

6. The behavioral change and the restoration of ecological balance take time, but persistent action does make it happen. Change takes time. The balance is not restored overnight. However, as the successful restoration of the polluted lakes and cleaner air in polluted cities demonstrates, with persistent action the balance can be restored.

In the balanced-life struggle, we need patience too, as we are going to fall back into old ways. The key is to continue with the game plan and not feel defeated.

In the ancient teaching and language of Sanskrit, the word for health is *svastha* — which means "to stay in yourself." When we are in tune with the needs of the self and are taking action to meet those needs on a regular basis, then we enjoy the real health — physical, mental and spiritual.

Some other lessons nature teaches us: If the root system of a tree is healthy, then it can withstand the loss of a few limbs, and over time, replace those limbs with healthy ones. If what is beneath the surface is healthy, then what is above the surface can take some shocks and still survive. The balanced lifestyle helps in developing a stronger internal system, which helps us withstand the shocks of the external world.

> *The balanced lifestyle helps in developing a stronger internal system, which helps us withstand the shocks of the external world.*

Another example of this phenomenon is a deep lake versus a shallow lake. If you throw a piece of rock in a shallow lake, the ripples on the surface are wider and last longer. But the same piece of rock in a deeper lake causes shorter ripples and settles in quietly. The deeper lake can withstand the "intrusion" of the rock with less disturbance than the shallow one.

In nature, no two animals, trees, lakes or hills are alike. It is the diversity that makes nature so beautiful. The different color flowers and foliage give the landscape its vibrancy and glorious beauty. Similarly, it is the uniqueness of each individual around us that gives a family, a community, a nation and the world its vibrancy and beauty.

The national parks are glorious simply by being themselves. Yosemite has its own charm in terms of beautiful waterfalls and mountains. The Grand Canyon has its own charm and serenity. The beaches in Hawaii do not need any transformation from humankind to be inviting.

All nature asks is that it be left undisturbed. We drive or fly for hours to see and share this beauty. Similarly, we are in our beautiful and natural state when we are personally at peace.

The full beauty of the Grand Canyon or Niagara Falls only becomes visible when we step back and take in the big picture.

Similarly, to appreciate life, from time to time we have to step back and take in the big picture.

By taking time for the four seasons — Spring, Summer, Fall and Winter — nature celebrates itself in its fullness. Let us celebrate life in its fullness by taking time for the four selves — Career, People, Actualizing and Leisure!

I Believe

I believe in the Creator:

Because of Glorious Sunrises
 Majestic Mountains
 Green Forests
 Blue Oceans
 and Other Wonders of Nature;

Because of Norman Vincent Peale
 Mahatma Gandhi
 Martin Luther King Jr.
 Mother Teresa
 and Other Spiritual Souls;

Because of Cornfields
 Quiet Moments
 Apple Orchards
 Sounds of Laughter
 and Other Life-Supporting Elements;

Because of Love
 Affection
 Forgiveness
 Compassion
 and Other Qualities of the Human Spirit;

Because of Pine Tree Scents after Rain
   Refreshing Landscapes after Snow
   Act of Holding Hands
   Family Picnics
   and Other Simple Pleasures of Life

Because of My Life Companion
   Parents
   Sisters and Brothers
   Innocent Little faces
   and Others in My Life Who Make Me Belong

Because, by Believing in the Supreme Being,
   I feel good about my own being.
   The stronger my belief grows,
   the closer I get to learning
   the art of leading a fuller life.

But, most of all, I believe in the Creator,
because I ask and receive peace of mind
   in this fast-paced lifestyle;

Because I feel this Dynamic Creative Life Force
   helping me toward the purpose of life,
   Celebration of Life in its Fullness.

The beauty in a flower does not cease to exist just because we are too busy to appreciate it. It waits for us. Similarly, the human spirit — the inner beauty, the inner force — waits for us to discover, appreciate and put it to use.

Balanced Life Checkup

*Not in the clamor of the crowded street, not in the shouts and plau-
dits of the throng, but in ourselves are triumph and defeat.*
— Henry Wadsworth Longfellow

FOLLOWING IS AN EXERCISE, a Balanced Life checkup to help
you apply the lessons discussed in the previous chapters. Just like
a medical checkup, the Balanced Life checkup will help you determine if everything is OK. If it is, then continue with your present
lifestyle. If it is not, then we need to make some changes.

Self-awareness is the first essential step toward making productive changes in achieving Balanced Life. Answers to the following questions will help you determine the areas of opportunity for
greater career and personal success in your environment. For each
question, circle the appropriate number:

0 — Agree/true most of the time
1 — Sometimes agree/true about half of the time
2 — Disagree/true very rarely

Scoring

The maximum number of points you can score in each category is 20. There is no magic number that says your life is in perfect balance. The objective of this checkup is to see, at this point in
time, which part of your life is not receiving the needed attention.

Rank the four scores from the highest to the lowest. The Self
category at the bottom of the list is the one that, at this stage in your
life, needs more of your time and energy.

Each statement with a score of 0 also provides some clue to understanding the thought process or activity that is contributing to the imbalance. The key is getting started with changes in just one activity or thought process. Trying to change more than one area at a time increases the chances of frustration and thus makes it easier to revert to the old ways.

It is OK if you slip back to the old behavior or time allocation on a given day. What is important is that you recognize it and correct it the next day.

Balanced Life Checkup:
CAREER SELF

1.	Upon hearing of a new idea which I was not a part of, "I don't think it will work" is my first reaction.	0	1	2
2.	I feel more comfortable making every decision myself rather than delegating authority.	0	1	2
3.	I find myself taking excessive responsibilities because of my thinking that, "Only I can do it the way it should be done."	0	1	2
4.	I tend to blame others for my failures — on and off the job.	0	1	2
5.	I feel under-challenged or under-utilized in my present job.	0	1	2
6.	I feel that I used to be able to concentrate better (I grow inattentive in meetings and conversations, while driving, etc.)	0	1	2
7.	I find myself letting people know only when their work is unsatisfactory, not when they have done a good job.	0	1	2
8.	The thought, "Looks like I am on a dead-end street in my present job/ occupation," crosses my mind.	0	1	2
9.	I get concerned about living in the fast lane.	0	1	2

10. Worrying about what might be   0   1   2
    affects my performance today.

                                    TOTAL _____

Balanced Life Checkup:
PEOPLE SELF

1. I find it hard to share my true feelings   0   1   2
   and self doubts with my spouse
   or significant other or best friend.

2. People in my life mention that I had   0   1   2
   more time for them when
   I did not make as much money.

3. I find it hard to forget the job after   0   1   2
   work hours and to be all there with my
   family.

4. I try to dominate every conversation,   0   1   2
   rather than listening and learning from
   others.

5. I get upset when my spouse or   0   1   2
   significant other accepts party invitations
   or makes plans that upset my routine.

6. I find it difficult to list five people who   0   1   2
   seek my company just for the fun of it.

7. Whether it's where to eat, what movie   0   1   2
   to see, where to go on vacation, the kind
   of house to buy, etc., I insist on having the
   final word on everything.

8. During the last six months, I have noticed a lack of interest or pleasure in sex on my part.   0   1   2

9. After a rough day at work, I do not normally bounce back by telling her or him, "As long as I have you, I can handle it".   0   1   2

10. I spend time with friends with whom I compete socially or occupationally.   0   1   2

TOTAL _____

Balanced Life Checkup:
ACTUALIZING SELF
(Inner Harmony / Inner Peace)

1. I make good money and have a happy home and social life, but feel something is missing.   0   1   2

2. I find myself preoccupied with looking forward to achieving goals in the future or to the things I don't have.   0   1   2

3. The quality of my People Life (relationships) is not what I want it to be.   0   1   2

4. There are parts of me (interests, skills, etc.) that don't get a chance to be expressed.   0   1   2

5. I don't feel I'm spiritually stronger than what I was a year ago.   0   1   2

6.   Because of the struggle to achieve more   0   1   2
     and more in less and less time, I have not
     been able to help someone less fortunate
     or do volunteer work.

7.   The quality of my career, in terms of   0   1   2
     what I want from it, is not there.

8.   I need tranquilizers, drinks and/or   0   1   2
     antacids to help me get through the
     day or night.

9.   I don't feel I'm becoming the kind of   0   1   2
     person I am capable of becoming
     — a successful human being.

10. The quality of my leisure life is driven   0   1   2
     more by career considerations and others
     than by me.

                              TOTAL_____

Balanced Life Checkup:
LEISURE/RECREATION SELF
(Health)

1.   I like to pursue my leisure/recreation   0   1   2
     interests, but cannot find the time or
     energy on a regular basis.

2.   My reading is related to work.   0   1   2

3.   When playing a sport, I am hard on   0   1   2
     myself, making it difficult to relax and
     enjoy.

4. I tell myself, "Let me get that next   0   1   2
    position ... or make that much more
    money ... and then I will slow down
    and enjoy life."

5. For no obvious reason, I feel depressed.   0   1   2

6. I find it hard just doing nothing.   0   1   2

7. My reaction to the question,   0   1   2
    "Are you getting what you want out
    of life?" is: "I'm so busy paying bills,
    I don't have time to think."

8. I don't know what is the matter, but I   0   1   2
    just can't get a kick out of anything
    anymore.

9. After a rough day at work, I do not   0   1   2
    normally bounce back by engaging in
    a leisure/recreation activity.

10. I feel indispensable and thus find it   0   1   2
    very difficult to take my vacation
    when I would really like to.

                                  TOTAL_____

CLOSING THOUGHTS

Attaining balanced life is a lot like cleaning out closets, according to business consultant Elizabeth Jefferies. When you bring home a brand-new suit or dress and stuff it into a closet already crowded with old, worn-out garments, the new one either gets badly wrinkled or, worse yet, becomes lost and forgotten in the crush of junk!

If you have gained a new idea or insight from reading this book or doing the self-assessment, treat it like a new suit or outfit that you have received as a special gift. Clean out your closet and make room for this new part of your wardrobe. Some of your old clothes (out-of-date ideas or habits) need to be thrown away entirely to make room for the new addition.

Other items (such as relationships) will blend well with the new addition if they are simply altered or repaired. Finally, some things (activities, for example) may need to be boxed up and stored, as they are not suitable for your lifestyle now, but are too precious to be thrown away entirely.

The co-author recalls doing some closet-cleaning at one point in order to make room (time) to complete this book! Some small amounts of space were created by discarding evening television. Several items required repair/refurbishing, such as asking the children to share more home responsibilities and working with Madan to redistribute responsibilities for the manuscript.

An addiction to heirloom sewing was carefully boxed up and stored in the attic until the book was finished. This was not an easy or painless process — as my family and co-workers can attest! However, the closet cleaning and life balancing were rewarded by being able to learn, grow and have fun in the process of creating this book.

• • •

Like closets, our lives need attention on a very regular basis. In paying careful attention to your own life, you do not just enrich yourself. You also become the unique gift to others that you were meant to be on the day you were born.

The gift is there. Unlock it. Enjoy it. Pass it on!

Learn More About
Balanced Life

If you would like to receive information on:

- Ordering additional copies

- Guest speakers for your meeting, conference and/or retreat

- Adding your name to the mailing list for forth-coming Balanced Life publications

Please send you name and address to:

The Balance Group
Suite 104
1160 West Poplar Avenue
Collierville, TN 38017